LONGMAN
SCIENCE

WORKBOOK

Longman

Longman Science
Workbook

Thanks to Roberto E. Yarzagaray for his contribution.

Pearson Education, 10 Bank Street, White Plains, NY 10606

Vice president, primary and secondary editorial: Ed Lamprich
Senior development editor: Lauren Weidenman
Development editor: Deborah Maya Lazarus
Editorial coordinator: Johnnie Farmer
Editorial assistant: Emily Lippincott
Vice president, director of production and design: Rhea Banker
Production supervisor: Christine Edmonds
Production editor: Laurie Neaman
Vice president, marketing: Kate McLoughlin
Senior marketing manager: Don Wulbrecht
Senior manufacturing buyer: Nancy Flaggman
Cover design: Rhea Banker
Text design and composition: Quarasan
Text font: 11/14 ITC Franklin Gothic Book
Credits: See page 113.

LONGMAN ON THE WEB

Longman.com offers online resources for
teachers and students. Access our Companion
Websites, our online catalog, and our local
offices around the world.

Visit us at **longman.com**.

ISBN: 0-13-193031-1

Printed in the United States of America
3 4 5 6 7 8 9 10–BAH–09 08 07

Contents

Name _____ Date _____

Getting Started: Introduction

What Is Science?

A. Match the parts of the sentence. Write the letter.

___c___ **1.** Science   **a.** is the earth and all things on it.

_____ **2.** Scientists   **b.** are things that are alive.

_____ **3.** Living things   **c.** is the study of the natural world.

_____ **4.** Nonliving things   **d.** are people who study our world.

_____ **5.** The world   **e.** are things that are not alive.

B. Complete each sentence. Use words from the box.

1. _____ is the earth and all things on it.

2. _____ are people who study our world.

3. _____ is the study of the natural world.

4. _____ are things that are not alive.

5. _____ are things that are alive.

| Living things |
| Nonliving things |
| Science |
| Scientists |
| The world |

C. Write *living thing* or *nonliving thing* under each picture.

_____ _____ _____

The Sciences

A. Match the parts of the sentence. Write the letter.

_____d_____ Life science   **a.** is the study of nonliving matter.

_____ **1.** Earth science   **b.** is what living and nonliving things are made of.

_____ **2.** The environment   **c.** is usable power such as sound, light, or electricity.

_____ **3.** Matter   **d.** is the study of living things on the earth.

_____ **4.** Physical science   **e.** is the land, water, and air on the earth.

_____ **5.** Energy   **f.** is the study of the earth.

B. Write five sentences with words and phrases from the exercise above.

Example: _Life science is the study of living things on the earth._

1. _____

2. _____

3. _____

4. _____

5. _____

C. Circle the word or phrase that doesn't belong.

1. electricity   energy   (plants)   physical science

2. life science   rocks   animals   plants

3. animals   earth science   rocks   land

4. environment   water   planets   air

5. energy   sound   light   rocks

6. living things   electricity   frogs   trees

Getting Started: Introduction

The Sciences

A. What kind of science does each picture show? Choose words from the box. Write the words under each picture.

| earth science   physical science   life science |

_____   _____   _____

_____   _____   _____

B. Complete the chart below. Write an example of each kind of science.

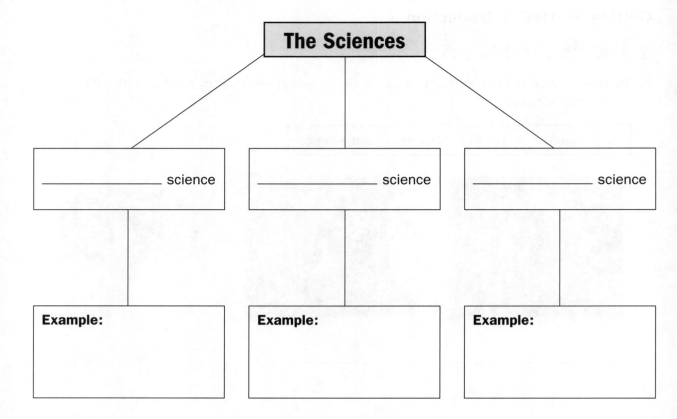

The Sciences

_____ science

_____ science

_____ science

Example:

Example:

Example:

C. Choose the best answer. Circle the letter.

1. _____ is the study of living things on the earth.

    a. Earth science   **b.** Physical science   **c.** Life science

2. The study of energy is part of _____.

    a. earth science   **b.** physical science   **c.** life science

3. Our _____ is the land, water, and air.

    a. living thing   **b.** environment   **c.** sun

4. _____ is the study of the earth.

    a. Earth science   **b.** Physical science   **c.** Life science

5. _____ is the study of nonliving matter.

    a. Earth science   **b.** Physical science   **c.** Life science

Name _____ Date _____

The Scientific Method

A. Write the steps of the scientific method in the correct order. Use the sentences from the box.

> - Draw conclusions.
> - Ask questions.
> - Test the hypothesis.
> - Make a hypothesis.
> - Observe.

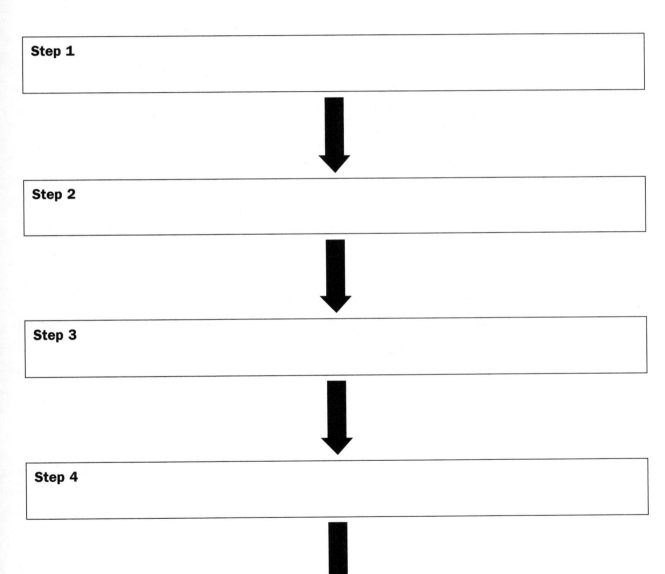

Step 1

Step 2

Step 3

Step 4

Step 5

B. Match the parts of the sentence. Write the letter.

_____ **1.** First, scientists ask questions

_____ **2.** After asking a question,

_____ **3.** After scientists make a hypothesis,

_____ **4.** Scientists observe

_____ **5.** Finally, when scientists draw conclusions,

a. scientists make a hypothesis.

b. very carefully to see what happens.

c. they decide if their hypothesis is correct.

d. about things they don't know.

e. they test their hypothesis.

C. Write five sentences with phrases from the exercise above.

1. _____

2. _____

3. _____

4. _____

5. _____

D. Write T for *true* or F for *false*.

_____ **1.** Scientists don't ask questions.

_____ **2.** A hypothesis is a guess.

_____ **3.** Scientists do experiments to test a hypothesis.

_____ **4.** First scientists draw conclusions, then they make a hypothesis.

_____ **5.** Observing is not part of the scientific method.

Getting Started: Introduction

Safety

A. Match each safety rule with a picture. Write the letter.

Safety Rules

a. Clean up spills.

b. Be careful with scissors.

c. Make sure you understand.

d. Be careful with electricity.

e. Be careful with hot things.

f. Keep things clean.

g. Stay away from broken glass.

h. Tell your teacher if you hurt yourself.

_____

_____

_____

_____

_____

_____

_____

_____

B. Match the parts of the sentence. Write the letter.

_____ **1.** Keep   **a.** if anything spills on the floor.

_____ **2.** Stay away   **b.** with scissors.

_____ **3.** Tell your teacher   **c.** electrical cords are out of the way.

_____ **4.** Make sure   **d.** things clean.

_____ **5.** Be careful   **e.** from broken glass.

C. Write T for _true_ or F for _false_.

_____ **1.** Always point scissors away from your body.

_____ **2.** Pick up broken glass yourself.

_____ **3.** Don't put things away after an experiment.

_____ **4.** Don't use electrical items near water.

_____ **5.** Don't clean up spills.

D. Complete the paragraph. Use words from the box.

clean	teacher	understand	hot	electricity

     Safety is very important in the science classroom. You should learn these basic safety rules. Make sure you **(1)** _____ the experiment before you begin. Be careful with **(2)** _____ things. Be careful with **(3)** _____, too. Make sure the cords are out of the way. Keep the experiment area **(4)** _____. Tell your **(5)** _____ if you hurt yourself.

Getting Started: Introduction

Practicing the Scientific Method

Experiment Log: How Does Water Move Inside a Flower?

Follow the steps of the scientific method as you do your experiment. Write notes about each step as the experiment progresses.

Step 1: Ask questions.

Step 2: Make a hypothesis.

Draw a picture here of the flowers before the experiment.

Step 3: Test your hypothesis.

Step 4: Observe.

Draw a picture here of the flowers after the experiment.

Step 5: Draw conclusions.

Getting Started: Introduction

Science Tools

VOCABULARY

A. Write the correct word under each picture. Use words from the box.

camera	hand lens	stopwatch
thermometer	microscope	balance

1. _____

2. _____

3. _____

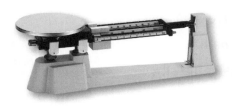

4. _____

5. _____

6. _____

B. Match the parts of the sentence. Write the letter.

_____ **1.** A ruler   **a.** lets you see small things close up.

_____ **2.** A hand lens   **b.** lets you see very small things.

_____ **3.** A balance   **c.** lets you measure how hot or cold something is.

_____ **4.** A telescope   **d.** lets you take pictures.

_____ **5.** A stopwatch   **e.** lets you measure how long something is.

_____ **6.** A thermometer   **f.** lets you see things far away.

_____ **7.** A camera   **g.** lets you measure how heavy something is.

_____ **8.** A microscope   **h.** lets you measure time.

C. Write eight sentences with words and phrases from the exercise above.

1. _____

2. _____

3. _____

4. _____

5. _____

6. _____

7. _____

8. _____

D. Complete each sentence. Use words from the box.

thermometer	microscope	telescope	hand lens	ruler

1. A _____ has centimeters and inches.

2. You hold a _____ in your hand to observe small things.

3. A _____ measures how hot or cold something is.

4. You look through a _____ to see things in the sky.

5. You can observe very, very small things with a _____.

Getting Started: Introduction

Visuals

Write the name of the visual under each picture. Use words from the box.

photograph	cycle diagram	diagram	pie chart
illustration	micrograph	chart	sectional diagram

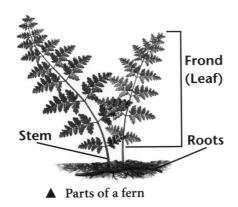

▲ Parts of a fern

1. _____   2. _____

3. _____

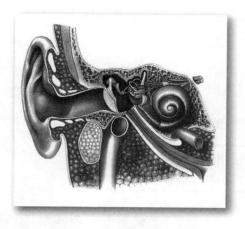

4. _____

5. _____

Matter	Speed of Sound	
	Meters per second	Feet per second
Dry, cold air	343	1,125
Water	1,550	5,085
Hard wood	3,960	12,992
Glass	4,540	14,895
Steel	5,050	16,568

6. _____

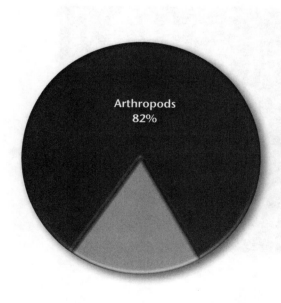

7. _____

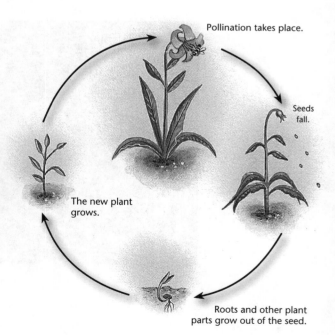

Pollination takes place.

Seeds fall.

The new plant grows.

Roots and other plant parts grow out of the seed.

8. _____

Name _____ Date _____

Getting Started: Introduction

More Review and Practice

Complete the puzzle. Use words from the box.

balance	microscope
energy	nonliving things
environment	science
hypothesis	stopwatch
life science	world
matter	

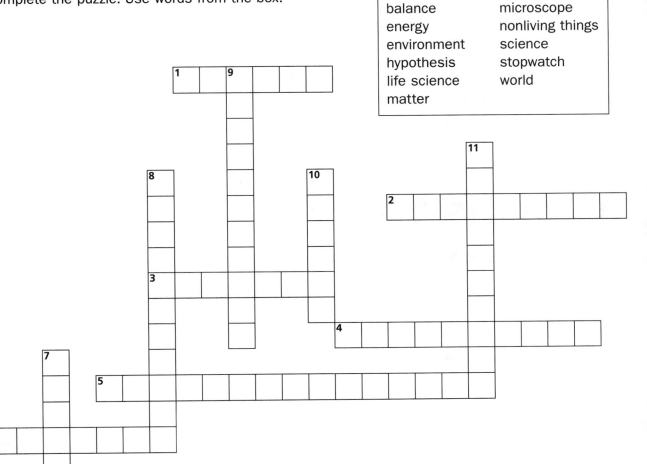

ACROSS

1. usable power
2. measures time
3. the study of the natural world
4. lets you see very small things
5. things that are not alive
6. measures how heavy something is

DOWN

7. Earth and all things on it
8. the study of living things
9. land, water, and air on the earth
10. what living and nonliving things are made of
11. a guess

CHECK YOUR UNDERSTANDING

Write T for *true* or F for *false*.

_______ **1.** Scientists use visuals to share information.

_______ **2.** Physical science is the study of living matter.

_______ **3.** Never tell your teacher if you hurt yourself.

_______ **4.** Life science is the study of living things on the earth.

_______ **5.** The scientific method has five important steps.

_______ **6.** A balance measures how hot something is.

_______ **7.** Safety is not important in the science classroom.

_______ **8.** You draw conclusions after an experiment.

_______ **9.** Earth science includes the study of our environment.

_______ **10.** A hypothesis is always correct.

APPLY SCIENCE SKILLS

Science Reading Strategy: Preview and Predict

Look at the pictures on page 2 in your Student Book. Then answer the questions.

1. What do the pictures show?

____

2. Which picture shows living things?

____

3. Which picture shows a nonliving thing?

____

4. Predict what you will learn about in your science book.

____

____

____

Unit 1: Lesson 1

Before You Read

VOCABULARY

A. Draw an arrow from each key word to its function.

leaves	take in water for the plant
1. petals	make food for the plant
2. roots	holds water and nutrients
3. seeds	holds the plant up
4. stem	can grow into new plants
5. soil	protect the inner parts of a flower

B. Write five sentences using the key word and its function.

Example: _Leaves make food for the plant._ _____

1. _____

2. _____

3. _____

4. _____

5. _____

C. Circle the best word to complete each sentence.

1. The roots grow deep in the (stem / soil).

2. (Petals / Seeds) can grow into a new plant.

3. The plant makes food in the (roots / leaves).

4. The (leaves / petals) protect the inner parts of the flower.

5. (Roots / Petals) take in water for the plant.

D. Write T for *true* or F for *false*.

_____ **1.** The stem holds the plant up.

_____ **2.** The leaves can grow into a new plant.

_____ **3.** Roots take in water from the soil.

_____ **4.** The stem protects the flower.

_____ **5.** The petals make food for the plant.

Science Reading Strategy: Main Idea and Details

Read the paragraph below. Write the main idea and details in the chart.

Insects and other animals are very important to plants. Plants produce flowers that attract insects. Insects pollinate the plants. This helps the flowers turn into fruits. Seeds are inside each fruit. Animals eat the fruit. They drop the seeds in the soil. This helps the seeds grow in new places.

Main Idea:

Detail:

Detail:

Detail:

Detail:

Unit 1: Lesson 1

Before You Read

SCIENCE SKILLS

Using Visuals: Diagrams

A. Look at the diagram. Answer the questions. Write complete sentences.

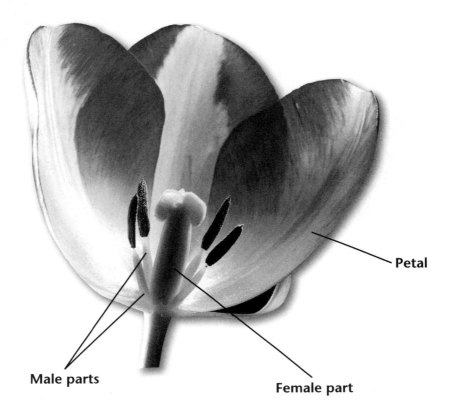

Petal

Male parts

Female part

1. What is a diagram?

   _____

2. What does this diagram show?

   _____

3. How many labeled parts do you see? Name them.

   _____

4 How does this diagram help you learn about plants?

   _____

5. What title can you give to this diagram?

   _____

B. Look at the two diagrams. Choose the best answer. Circle the letter.

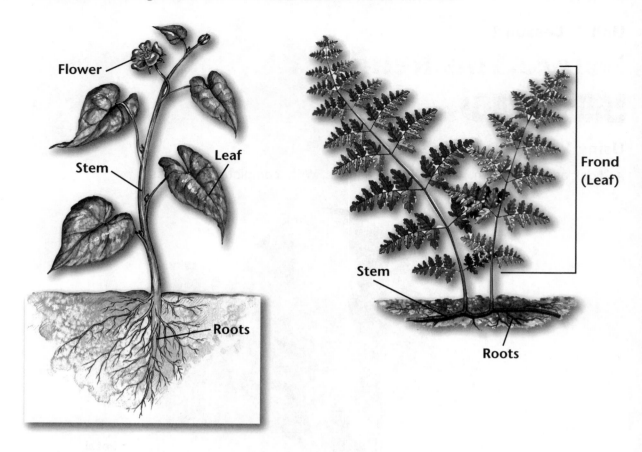

1. Look at the plant on the left. It is a _____.

    a. fern   **b.** cactus   **c.** flowering plant

2. One trait the plants in the diagrams share is _____ leaves.

    a. green   **b.** thin   **c.** tiny

3. One trait the plants in the diagrams *don't* share is _____.

    a. roots   **b.** flowers   **c.** stems

4. These plants both have _____.

    a. fruit   **b.** flowers   **c.** roots

5. Both plants _____ their own food.

    a. make   **b.** grow   **c.** cook

Unit 1: Lesson 1

More Review and Practice

VOCABULARY

Complete the sentences. Use words from the box.

| leaves |
| petals |
| roots |
| soil |
| stem |

1. Flowers have _____.

2. Roots grow deep in the _____.

3. _____ make food for the plant.

4. A _____ carries water to the leaves.

5. _____ take in water and nutrients.

VOCABULARY IN CONTEXT

Complete the paragraph. Use words from the box.

| seeds | roots | leaves | stems | soil |

A farmer needs rich **(1)** _____ to grow plants. Most plants start life as

(2) _____. Then they grow **(3)** _____ deep in the ground.

Next they grow **(4)** _____ to hold the plant up. After that they develop

(5) _____ to make their own food. Later, plants grow flowers.

CHECK YOUR UNDERSTANDING

Circle the best answer to complete each sentence.

1. The stem carries _____ to the leaves.

   a. trees   **b.** water   **c.** soil

2. Plants use their _____ to make food.

   a. roots   **b.** leaves   **c.** stems

3. Most plants have four parts: _____, roots, and leaves.

   a. nutrients, flowers   **b.** soil, water   **c.** flowers, stems

4. The female part of a flower becomes a _____.

   a. fruit   **b.** root   **c.** stem

5. Plants take in and give off _____.

   a. light   **b.** needles   **c.** gases

Science Reading Strategy: Main Idea and Details

Read the paragraph. Write the main idea and details in the chart.

The stem does many things for a plant. It holds the plant up. It also holds up the plant's leaves. This lets the sun shine on them. The stem carries water and food from place to place inside the plant.

Main Idea:

Detail:	Detail:	Detail:

Using Visuals: Diagrams

Look at the diagram. Write the labels on the lines.

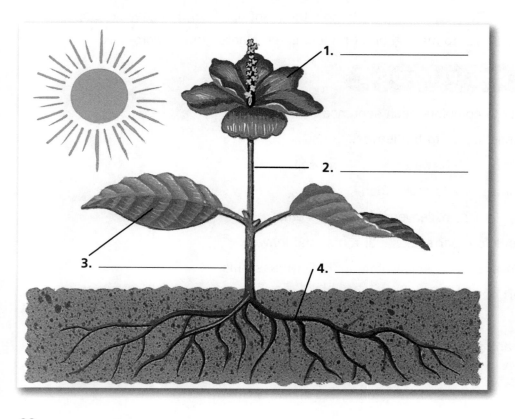

1. _____

2. _____

3. _____

4. _____

Unit 1: Lesson 2

Before You Read

VOCABULARY

A. Draw an arrow from each key word to words that tell about it.

1. pollination	how a plant makes food
2. germination	heat and light
3. photosynthesis	small animals such as bees and butterflies
4. pollen	passing pollen from flower to flower
5. energy	yellow powder on a male flower part
6. insects	a new plant beginning to grow from a seed

B. Write four sentences using a key word and words that tell about it.

1. _____

2. _____

3. _____

4. _____

C. Write T for *true* or F for *false*.

_____ **1.** Plants use energy in light to make food.

_____ **2.** Plants do not need to make food.

_____ **3.** Insects carry seeds from flower to flower.

_____ **4.** Germination occurs when a new plant begins to grow.

_____ **5.** Plants move to find food.

D. Match words on the left with the sentences on the right. Write the letter.

_____ **1.** pollination   **a.** It is often yellow.

_____ **2.** germination   **b.** They are kinds of energy.

_____ **3.** pollen   **c.** Plants use this process to make food.

_____ **4.** heat and light   **d.** A plant begins to grow from a seed.

_____ **5.** photosynthesis   **e.** Insects pass pollen from flower to flower.

Science Reading Strategy: Compare and Contrast

A. Read this text. As you read, look for sentences that tell what is the same or what is different about these two plants.

Both the water lily and the cactus belong to the plant kingdom. A water lily grows in fresh water. A cactus grows in the desert. A water lily has broad and flat leaves. A cactus's leaves are long and thin. They are called spines, and they protect the plant. They save more water than broad and flat leaves. A water lily has stems underwater. A cactus has stems above the ground. Both plants have roots. They both use photosynthesis to make food, and they both have flowers.

B. Write information in the Venn diagram to compare and contrast the water lily and the cactus.

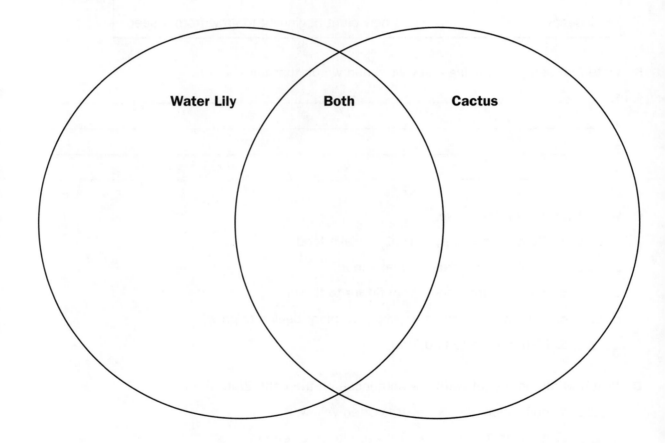

Water Lily　　　**Both**　　　**Cactus**

Name _____ Date _____

Unit 1: Lesson 2

Before You Read

Science Reading Strategy: Compare and Contrast

Read the paragraph about apples and papayas. Then write how they are alike and how they are different in the Venn diagram below.

   Apples and papayas are both fruits. They are sweet, juicy, and good to eat. They both contain seeds. But apples and papayas are different in some ways. Apples are mostly round in shape. Papayas are shaped more like pears. The flesh—the part that we eat—of a ripe apple is hard. The flesh of a ripe papaya is soft. In general, apples grow in cool climates. Papayas grow in warm climates.

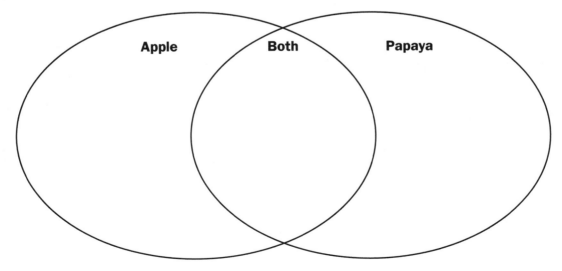

Apple   Both   Papaya

Using Visuals: Cycle Diagrams

You have just learned about the life cycle of an apple tree. Look at the diagram again. Then answer the questions.

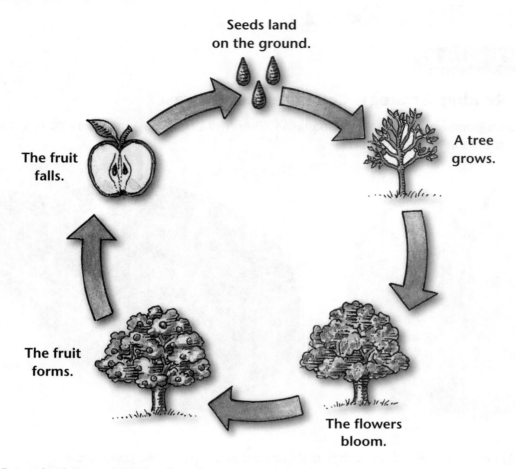

1. Where do the seeds come from?

   _____

2. What happens to the seeds?

   _____

3. What happens after the tree grows?

   _____

4. Do flowers bloom after the fruit forms or before?

   _____

5. What happens to the fruit?

   _____

Name _____ Date _____

Unit 1: Lesson 2
More Review and Practice

VOCABULARY

Use words from the box to identify each clue. Write the word on the line. There is one extra word.

| photosynthesis | germination | energy |
| pollen | insects | pollination |

1. It is the process by which a plant makes food. _____
2. Plants get this from the sun. _____
3. Insects carry it from flower to flower. _____
4. It is the process of new plants growing from seeds. _____
5. It is the process of passing pollen from flower to flower. _____

VOCABULARY IN CONTEXT

Rewrite the sentences that are *false*.

Example: The male parts of a flower make **insects**.

The male parts of a flower make pollen.

1. **Pollination** is the process plants use to make food.

_____

2. Plants use **energy** from sunlight to make food.

_____

3. **Insects** carry pollen from flower to flower.

_____

4. The process of new plants growing from seeds is called **pollen**.

_____

5. **Photosynthesis** is when insects pass pollen from flower to flower.

_____

Choose the best answer. Circle the letter.

1. Plants change water and carbon dioxide into sugar and _____.

   a. energy   **b.** pollen   **c.** oxygen

2. _____ are inside the fruit.

   a. Pine cones   **b.** Seeds   **c.** Bees

3. _____ are helpful to plants. They help to pollinate.

   a. Insects   **b.** Flowers   **c.** Vegetables

4. The _____ part of the flower makes the pollen.

   a. female   **b.** male   **c.** petal

5. Inside a seed there is _____.

   a. carbon dioxide   **b.** fruit   **c.** a new plant and food

APPLY SCIENCE SKILLS

Science Reading Strategy: Compare and Contrast

Read the paragraph. Complete the Venn diagram below.

A lemon and a peach are different in some ways. But they are the same in some ways, too. A lemon has many small seeds. A peach has one big seed. A lemon tastes sour. Peaches taste sweet. Lemons and peaches are fruits. They both produce flowers, and they both begin life as seeds.

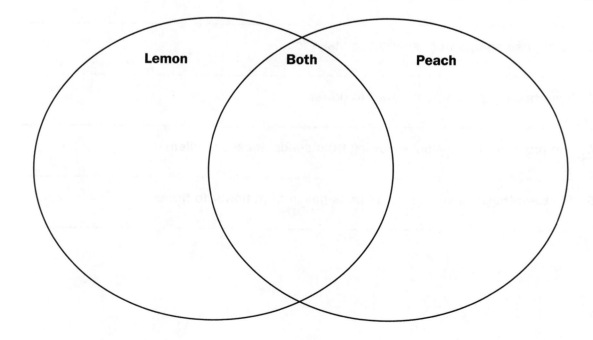

Unit 1
Unit Review

VOCABULARY

A. Match the key words on the left with the phrases on the right.

_____h_____   leaves   **a.** process of passing pollen from flower to flower

_____ **1.** pollination   **b.** protect the inner parts of a flower

_____ **2.** insects   **c.** a yellow powder

_____ **3.** roots   **d.** carry pollen from flower to flower

_____ **4.** petals   **e.** holds the plant up

_____ **5.** seeds   **f.** take in water and nutrients from the soil

_____ **6.** photosynthesis   **g.** are carried by wind, water, and animals

_____ **7.** germination   **h.** make food using sunlight

_____ **8.** pollen   **i.** comes from the sun

_____ **9.** stem   **j.** process of breaking out of a seed

_____ **10.** energy   **k.** process of making food in the leaves

B. Write 10 sentences with words and phrases from the exercise above.

Example: _Leaves make food using sunlight._ _____

1. _____

2. _____

3. _____

4. _____

5. _____

6. _____

7. _____

8. _____

9. _____

10. _____

Complete the paragraph. Use words from the box.

energy	germination	pollen	photosynthesis	insects

Plants need **(1)** _____ and other animals to carry **(2)** _____
from flower to flower. Plants get **(3)** _____ from the food they make.
(4) _____ is the process plants use to make their food. This process takes
place in the leaves. I learned that **(5)** _____ is when a new plant breaks out
of a seed.

APPLY SCIENCE SKILLS

Using Visuals: Diagrams

Look at the diagrams below. Label the parts of a plant. Label the parts of a flower.

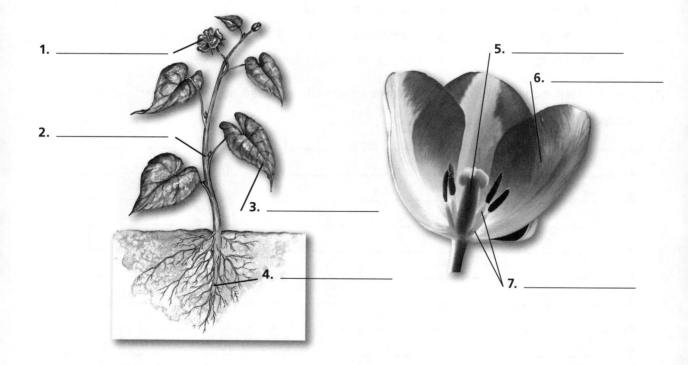

1. _____

2. _____

3. _____

4. _____

5. _____

6. _____

7. _____

EXTENSION PROJECT

Collect seeds from different kinds of plants. Label the seeds to tell what plants they come
from. Display your collection in the classroom.

Unit 1: Unit Experiment

Experiment Log: Do Plants Grow toward the Light?

Follow the steps of the scientific method as you do your experiment. Write notes about each step as the experiment progresses.

Step 1: Ask questions.

Step 2: Make a hypothesis.

Step 3: Test your hypothesis.

Step 4: Observe.

Step 5: Draw conclusions.

Write About It

1. Write about your favorite fruit. Where does it come from? What kind of tree does it grow on? What kind of seeds does it have?

2. Write about a plant that grows around your neighborhood. What kinds of leaves does it have? What kinds of flowers does it have? Does it have long or short stems? Do you like this plant? Why or why not?

Unit 2: Lesson 1

Before You Read

VOCABULARY

A. Draw an arrow from each key word to the words that tell about it.

1. survive	eats both plants and animals
2. traits	means to stay alive
3. carnivore	eats only plants
4. herbivore	facts about an animal
5. omnivore	eats only other animals

B. Write five sentences using each key word and the words that tell about it.

1. _____

2. _____

3. _____

4. _____

5. _____

C. Circle the best word to complete each sentence.

1. A (species / trait) is a specific kind of animal.

2. An (omnivore / herbivore) eats only plants.

3. A(n) (herbivore / carnivore) eats other animals.

4. Humans have a common (trait / carnivore) called hair.

5. An (herbivore / omnivore) eats both plants and animals.

6. Animals need water to (survive / trait).

D. Circle the word or phrase that doesn't belong.

1. lion	plants	herbivore	elephant
2. water	survive	food	species
3. survive	eight legs	hair	trait
4. omnivore	bear	horse	plants and animals

Science Reading Strategy: Use What You Know

A. Think about what you already know about cats. Write your ideas in the word web below.

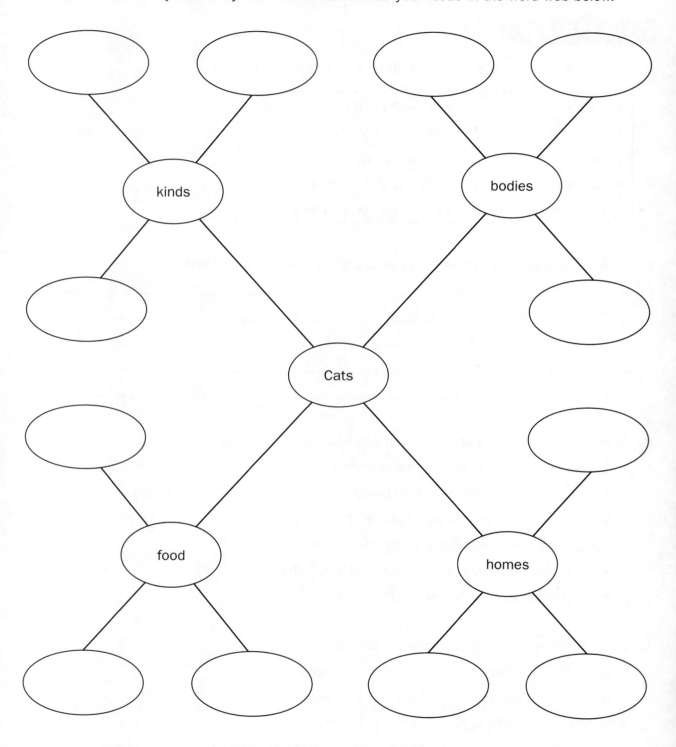

B. Compare your word web with a partner's. Add new information from your partner's word web to your own. Use a different-colored pen.

Unit 2: Lesson 1

Before You Read

SCIENCE SKILLS

Using Visuals: Photographs

Look at the photographs. Then answer the questions.

▲ A lioness

▲ An orangutan

1. Which animal is an herbivore? What is this animal doing?

_____

_____

2. Which animal is a carnivore? What is this animal doing?

_____

_____

3. What traits do these animals share?

_____

_____

4. Which animal needs to move faster to get food? Why?

_____

_____

Using Visuals: Photographs

Look at the photograph. Choose the best answer. Circle the letter.

1. Look at the food on the table. These people are probably _____.

    a. herbivores   **b.** carnivores   **c.** omnivores

2. One common trait you can see in the photograph is _____.

    a. a table   **b.** hair   **c.** tails

3. These people are probably in a _____.

    a. restaurant   **b.** house   **c.** car

4. These people are probably from the same _____.

    a. family   **b.** school   **c.** workplace

5. The people in the picture probably _____ their food.

    a. hunt   **b.** plant   **c.** buy

Unit 2: Lesson 1

More Review and Practice

VOCABULARY

Complete the puzzle. Use key words. Write the secret word.

1. An _____ eats only plants.

2. Animals cannot _____ without water.

3. An _____ eats plants and animals.

4. Human _____ include eye color and hair color.

5. A _____ eats only meat.

Secret word: ___ ___ ___ ___ ___

VOCABULARY IN CONTEXT

Complete the paragraph. Use words from the box. There is one extra word.

survive	trait	omnivores	herbivores	species	carnivores

At the Saint Louis Zoo, workers prepare food for the many **(1)** _____
of animals. The kind of food an animal eats is a **(2)** _____ of that animal.
The workers need to prepare meat for the **(3)** _____. They need to find
plants for the **(4)** _____. The food must be prepared 365 days a year so
the animals can **(5)** _____.

CHECK YOUR UNDERSTANDING

Choose the best answer. Circle the letter.

1. Animals need _____ to survive.

   a. trees and flowers   **b.** water and shelter   **c.** oxygen and gills

2. Animals _____ to find food and get away from danger.

   a. grow   **b.** hide   **c.** move

3. Fish breathe through their _____.

   a. lungs   **b.** gills   **c.** mouth

4. A woodpecker's long beak is an example of _____.

   a. an adaptation   **b.** a shelter   **c.** an herbivore

Science Reading Strategy: Use What You Know

Think about what you already know about birds. Write your ideas in the word web below.

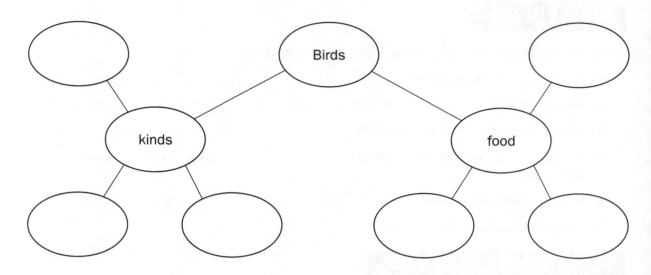

Using Visuals: Photographs

Look at the photograph. Then answer the questions.

1. Do you think this bird lives near water?
Why or why not?

_____

_____

2. Look at this bird's beak. Describe its shape.

_____

_____

3. Why do you think this bird has a long neck?

_____

_____

4. Name some other traits this bird has.

_____

_____

5. How do you think this bird moves?

_____

_____

▲ Flamingo

Unit 2: Lesson 2

Before You Read

VOCABULARY

A. Draw an arrow from each key word to words that tell about it.

1. communicate	animals without backbones
2. amphibians	use bodies and sounds
3. reptiles	animals such as frogs
4. invertebrates	animals such as dogs and humans
5. mammals	animals such as snakes and lizards

B. Write five sentences below using each key word and words that tell about it.

1. _____

2. _____

3. _____

4. _____

5. _____

C. Write T for *true* or F for *false*.

_____ **1.** Amphibians are born on land.

_____ **2.** Mammals have backbones.

_____ **3.** All species can communicate.

_____ **4.** Jellyfish are vertebrates.

_____ **5.** Reptiles are invertebrates.

D. Match the parts of the sentence. Write the letter.

_____ **1.** Animals with backbones are called   **a.** mammals.

_____ **2.** Animals that begin life in the water are   **b.** reptiles.

_____ **3.** Animals with no backbones are called   **c.** vertebrates.

_____ **4.** Animals that have fur or hair and feed   **d.** amphibians.
milk to their young are
    e. invertebrates.

_____ **5.** Snakes, turtles, and lizards are

Science Reading Strategy: Key Sentences

A. Read the paragraph. Look for key sentences about zebras. Underline the key sentences.

All zebras are mammals. They live in Africa. There are three species of zebras—plains, Grevy's, and mountain. All zebra species have stripes. The stripes are a little different for each species. Zebras are herbivores. They eat grass and spend most of their time grazing. They move from place to place looking for food.

B. Complete the chart. Write four key sentences from the paragraph about zebras.

Zebras = ⬚ + ⬚ + ⬚

\+ ⬚

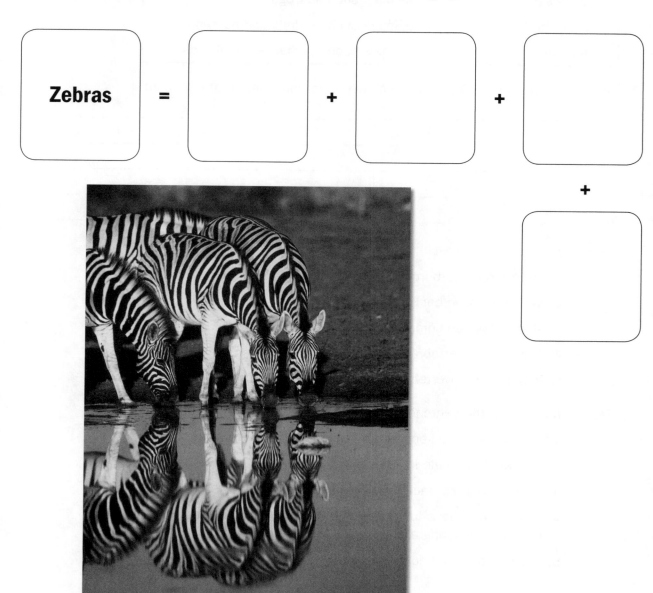

Unit 2: Lesson 2

Before You Read

SCIENCE SKILLS

Using Visuals: Pie Charts

This pie chart shows the different species of zebras in Africa. Look at the pie chart.
Then answer the questions.

**Zebra Population in Africa
(estimated)**

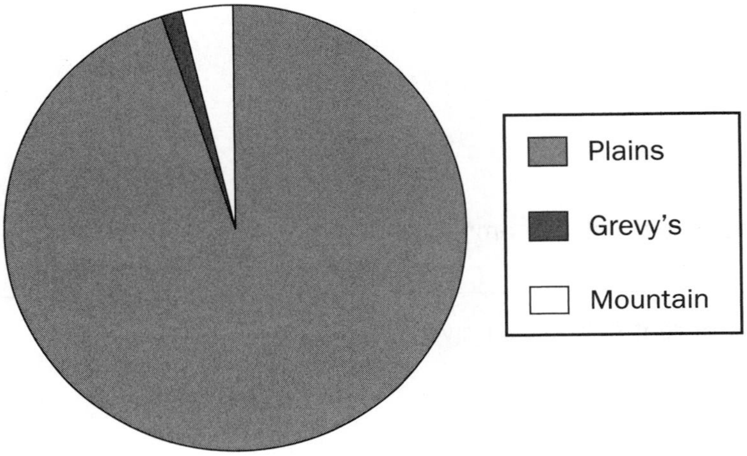

Legend:
- Plains
- Grevy's
- Mountain

1. How many species of zebras does this pie chart show?

   _____

2. Which species has the largest number of zebras?

   _____

3. Which species has the smallest number of zebras?

   _____

4. What percent of zebras in Africa does the pie chart show?

   _____

5. Which species do you think is endangered? Why?

   _____

Using Visuals: Pie Charts

This pie chart shows information about different species of fish in the reefs around Puerto Rico. Look at the pie chart. Then answer the questions.

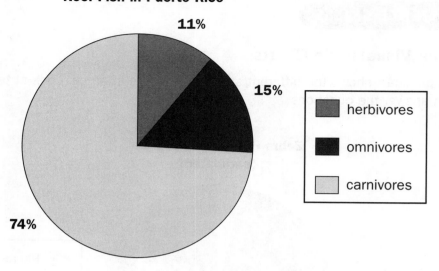

Reef Fish in Puerto Rico

11%

15%

74%

herbivores

omnivores

carnivores

1. What percent of reef fish are omnivores?

_____

2. What percent of reef fish are carnivores?

_____

3. What percent of reef fish are herbivores?

_____

4. What percent are the omnivores and herbivores together?

_____

5. Which group is the largest?

_____

Unit 2: Lesson 2

More Review and Practice

VOCABULARY

Use words from the box to identify each clue. Write the word on the line.

| mammals | reptiles | amphibians | vertebrates | invertebrates |

1. They have scales and lungs, and they lay eggs. _____

2. They have fur or hair and lungs. _____

3. They have a soft body and no backbone. _____

4. They have gills and fins when they are born. _____

5. They have a backbone. _____

VOCABULARY IN CONTEXT

Write T for *true* or F for *false.*

_____ 1. Frogs are amphibians.

_____ 2. Animals cannot communicate with each other.

_____ 3. All mammals use gills to breathe.

_____ 4. All reptiles live on land.

_____ 5. Invertebrates have no backbones.

CHECK YOUR UNDERSTANDING

Choose the best answer. Circle the letter.

1. Fish are examples of _____.

   a. amphibians   **b.** mammals   **c.** vertebrates

2. Amphibians grow _____ when they are older.

   a. legs and lungs   **b.** gills and tails   **c.** gills and fins

3. Jellyfish, crabs, and spiders are examples of _____.

   a. vertebrates   **b.** invertebrates   **c.** reptiles

4. Mammal babies _____.

   a. have scales   **b.** hatch from eggs   **c.** drink mother's milk

5. Amphibians, reptiles, birds, fish, and mammals are all _____.

   a. invertebrates   **b.** vertebrates   **c.** species

Science Reading Strategy: Key Sentences

Reread the text about birds on page 85 in your Student Book. Write five key sentences that tell what traits birds have.

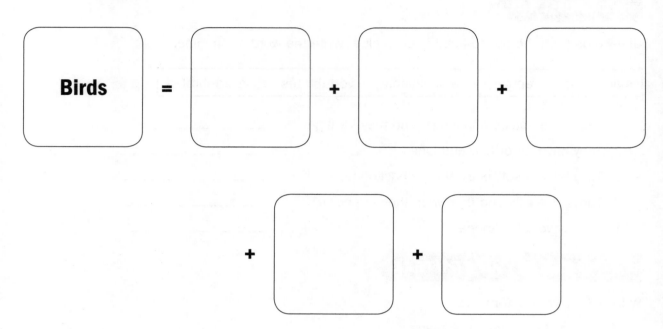

Using Visuals: Pie Charts

This pie chart shows the percent of endangered reptile species in the world. Look at the pie chart. Then answer the questions.

Reptiles

20% endangered

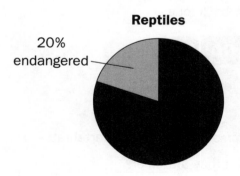

1. What percent of reptiles are endangered? _____

2. What percent of reptiles are not endangered? _____

3. Look at the pie charts on page 89 in your Student Book.

   a. Are reptiles more endangered than birds? _____

   b. Are reptiles more endangered than amphibians? _____

   c. Are reptiles more endangered than fish? _____

Unit 2

Unit Review

VOCABULARY

Draw an arrow from each key word to words that tell about it. Write sentences.

1. all species   have no backbones

2. carnivores   animals need water

3. reptiles   meat eaters

4. invertebrates   meat and plant eaters

5. amphibians   birth live young

6. mammals   scales or plates and lungs

7. to survive   communicate

8. omnivores   gills and fins at birth

1. _____

2. _____

3. _____

4. _____

5. _____

6. _____

7. _____

8. _____

VOCABULARY IN CONTEXT

Complete the paragraph. Use words from the box. There is one extra word.

survive	invertebrates	herbivores	omnivores	vertebrates	carnivores

Bears are **(1)** _____. They eat plants, but they also eat fish.

(2) _____ have sharp teeth. They eat meat. There are two main groups

of animals. **(3)** _____ make up 95% of the animal kingdom and

(4) _____ make up 5% of the animal kingdom. Animals need four things

to **(5)** _____: food, water, oxygen, and shelter.

Science Reading Strategy: Key Sentences

Read the paragraph. As you read, look for key sentences. Write four key sentences in the diagram.

Fish are the biggest group of vertebrates. There are 24,000 species of fish. All fish live in salt water or fresh water. Freshwater fish live in lakes, rivers, and streams. Saltwater fish live in the oceans. Many fish are endangered. There are more than 100 saltwater fish species on the Red List of endangered species. All fish need clean water, shelter, and food to survive.

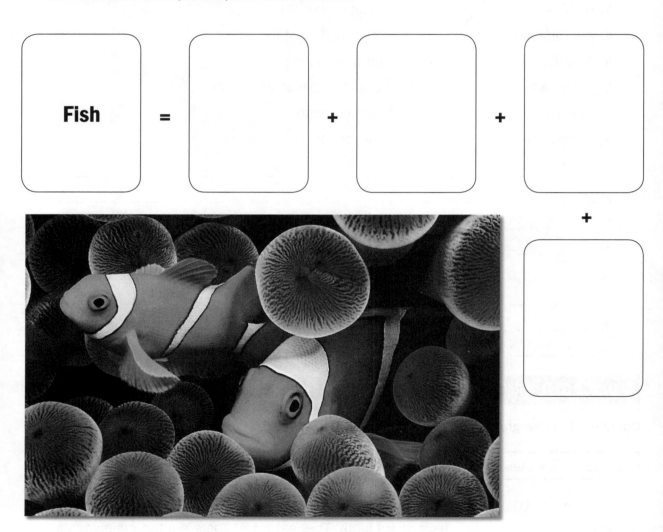

Fish = [ ] + [ ] + [ ]

+ [ ]

In this unit you learned about animal adaptations such as different kinds of teeth or beaks. Find out about other animal adaptations. Choose one adaptation and write a paragraph about it.

Unit 2: Unit Experiment

Experiment Log: What Traits Do Animals Share?

Follow the steps of the scientific method as you do your experiment. Write notes about each step as the experiment progresses.

Step 1: Ask questions.

Step 2: Make a hypothesis.

Step 3: Test your hypothesis.

Step 4: Observe.

Data Table	
Item	**Traits**

Step 5: Draw conclusions.

Write About It

1. Think about the animals you studied in this unit. What is your favorite group of animals? Mammals? Reptiles? Amphibians? Birds? Fish? Write a paragraph about your favorite group. Name some animals in this group and their traits.

_____
_____
_____
_____
_____
_____
_____
_____
_____

2. A very large tsunami hit Asia and parts of Africa on December 26, 2004. The wild animals survived, but many, many people died. How do you think animals know when there is danger? Use what you know about animals to write your ideas.

_____
_____
_____
_____
_____
_____
_____
_____
_____
_____

Unit 3: Lesson 1

Before You Read

VOCABULARY

A. Match each key word with words that tell about it. Write the letter.

_____ **1.** properties   **a.** rock made from hot liquid rock

_____ **2.** igneous   **b.** rock made from sand, mud, and pieces of rock

_____ **3.** metamorphic   **c.** traits

_____ **4.** mineral   **d.** rock made from rock that is changed by heat and pressure

_____ **5.** sedimentary   **e.** nonliving substance that rock is made of

B. Write five sentences using each key word and its definition.

1. _____

2. _____

3. _____

4. _____

5. _____

C. Circle the best word to complete each sentence.

1. A rock changed by heat and pressure is called a (trait / metamorphic) rock.

2. When a (diamond / volcano) erupts, hot liquid rock comes out of the ground.

3. (Igneous / Sedimentary) rock is made of sand, mud, and very small pieces of rock.

4. A diamond is made of one (metamorphic / mineral).

5. Rock made from hot liquid rock is (igneous / sedimentary) rock.

D. Write T for *true* or F for *false*. Correct the sentences that are false.

_____ **1.** A diamond is clear and soft.

_____ **2.** Metamorphic rock is rock changed by heat and pressure.

_____ **3.** Sedimentary rock is made from hot liquid rock.

_____ **4.** Igneous rock is dark.

_____ **5.** Hot liquid rock erupts out of a diamond.

Science Reading Strategy: Ask Questions

A. You just learned to ask questions as you read. Read the paragraph below. Write questions using *What, Where, Why,* and *How.* Then write your answers.

The earth has four layers. On the outermost layer is where we live. This layer is called the crust. The crust is like the shell of an egg. It is thin compared to the other layers. It is only 3–25 miles thick. The crust is made of lighter materials than the other layers. Heavier materials sink down, so they end up deep inside the earth.

Question Words	Questions and Answers
What	
Where	
Why	
How	

B. Now share your questions and answers with a partner.

Unit 3: Lesson 1
Before You Read

SCIENCE SKILLS

Science Reading Strategy: Ask Questions

A. Read the paragraph below. Write questions using *What, When, Where,* and *How.* Then write your answers.

Minerals have several common properties. They are found in the earth. They are nonliving. They are made up of specific groups of atoms. They are solid, and they have crystals. Minerals such as gold, silver, copper, and iron lie in the openings of ancient volcanoes. A very long time ago, humans discovered some of these minerals and used them to make tools.

Question Words	Questions and Answers
What	
When	
Where	
How	

B. Now share your questions and answers with a partner.

Using Visuals: Sectional Diagrams

Look at the sectional diagram of the earth's layers. Then answer the questions.

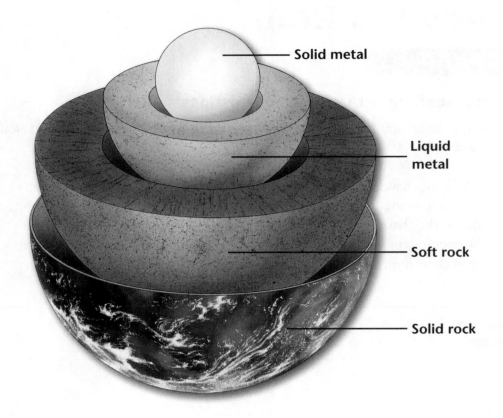

1. How many layers do you see in this sectional diagram?

   _____

2. What are the two inner layers made of?

   _____

3. What are the two outer layers made of?

   _____

4. Which layer is made of rock that is not solid?

   _____

5. Which layer is at the center of the earth?

   _____

Unit 3: Lesson 1

More Review and Practice

VOCABULARY

Complete the puzzle. Use key words. Write the secret word.

1. A mineral's traits are called _____.

2. Volcanoes make _____ rock.

3. Heat and pressure change rock into _____ rock.

4. Some _____ rock is made of sand.

5. A _____ erupts.

6. A diamond is made of one _____.

Secret word: ___ ___ ___ ___ ___ ___ (a kind of igneous rock)

VOCABULARY IN CONTEXT

Complete the paragraph. Use words from the box. There is one extra word.

igneous	volcano	sedimentary	metamorphic

A **(1)** _____ is a big mountain that erupts. Hot liquid rock comes out. When it cools, it forms **(2)** _____ rock. This rock can change. Heat and pressure can change it into **(3)** _____ rock.

CHECK YOUR UNDERSTANDING

Choose the best answer. Circle the letter.

1. Sedimentary rock is tiny pieces of rock, _____ joined together.

   a. mud, and sand   **b.** water, and halite   **c.** copper, and iron

2. The surface of the earth is called the _____.

   a. inner core   **b.** crust   **c.** mantle

3. About twenty kinds of _____ make up most of the earth's rocks.

   a. diamonds   **b.** liquids   **c.** minerals

4. The inner core is made of _____ metal.

   a. soft   **b.** liquid   **c.** solid

APPLY SCIENCE SKILLS

Science Reading Strategy: Ask Questions

Read the paragraph below. Write questions using *What, Why, Where,* and *How.* Then write your answers.

The earth has four layers. The first layer is the crust. This is the ground where you stand. Next to the crust is the mantle. It is made of hot, soft rock. Forces inside the earth push this soft rock up through a volcano's opening. The next layer is the outer core. It is made of liquid metal that flows continuously around the inner core. The inner core is made of solid metal. Scientists cannot go inside the last three layers to study them because they are too deep and too hot.

Question Words	Questions and Answers
What	
Why	
Where	
How	

Using Visuals: Sectional Diagrams

Look at the diagram on page 109 in your Student Book. Then answer the questions.

1. What does the diagram show?

2. What is coming out of the volcano?

3. What are two types of igneous rock in the diagram?

4. Can igneous rock be formed in any other way?

5. Do you think this volcano is active? Why or why not?

Unit 3: Lesson 2

Before You Read

VOCABULARY

A. Draw an arrow from each key word to words that tell about it.

1. weathering	the movement of rocks and soil
2. geologist	the breaking up of rock into pieces
3. erosion	a shaking of the ground
4. earthquake	a big sheet of ice
5. glacier	a person who studies rocks

B. Write five sentences using each key word and the words that tell about it.

1. _____

2. _____

3. _____

4. _____

5. _____

C. Write T for *true* or F for *false.* Correct the sentences that are false.

_____ **1.** An earthquake shakes the ground.

_____ **2.** Weathering is the study of weather.

_____ **3.** Geology is the study of rocks.

_____ **4.** Wind, water, and glaciers can cause geology.

_____ **5.** A glacier is a big sheet of sand.

D. Circle the word or phrase that doesn't belong.

1. wind	weathering	earthquake	water
2. geology	life science	rocks	geologist
3. earthquake	building	shake	sand
4. move	volcano	erosion	rocks
5. glacier	water	igneous	ice

Science Reading Strategy: Cause and Effect

A. Read the paragraph. As you read, look for cause and effect. Then answer the questions.

Heavy rain or an earthquake can cause a mudslide. Mudslides can cause severe damage to cities. In January 2004, in Ventura County, California, a big mudslide destroyed many houses and trees. The mudslide damaged roads, too. Several people died as a result of this mudslide.

1. What can heavy rain or an earthquake cause?

_____

2. What are some effects of a mudslide?

_____

B. Complete the diagram below. Write the effects in the circle on the right.

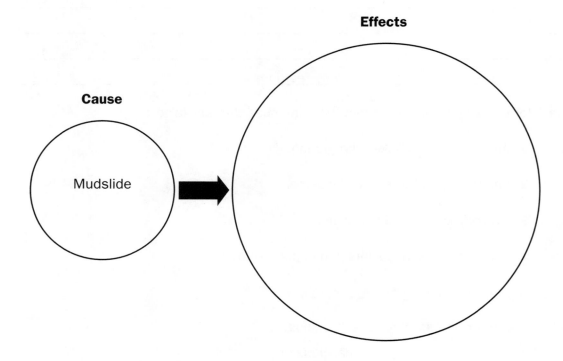

Cause

Mudslide

Effects

Unit 3: Lesson 2

Before You Read

SCIENCE SKILLS

Science Reading Strategy: Cause and Effect

A. Read the paragraph. As you read, look for cause and effect. Then answer the questions.

In some developing countries, people cut down a lot of trees. This is called deforestation. Deforestation has several bad effects on the land and the people who live on it. When there are no trees, strong rains can cause mudslides. Deforestation can also cause erosion of the soil. The soil moves because there are no tree roots to hold it down. Animals that live in the trees go to other locations. Soon the land is no longer useful to plants, animals, or humans.

1. What is deforestation?

_____

2. What causes soil erosion?

_____

B. Complete the diagram below. Write one effect in each box.

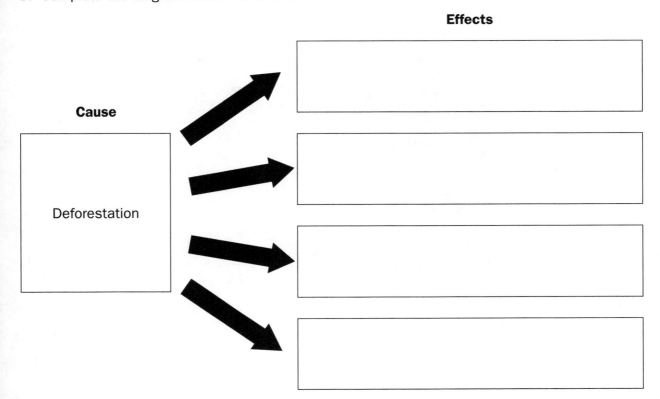

Effects

Cause

Deforestation

Using Visuals: Photo Sequences

A. You learned that a photo sequence shows an event in two or more photographs. Read the paragraph below.

> First the volcano erupts. Hot liquid rock comes out. Then the hot liquid rock cools and hardens, forming igneous rock. Over time, the igneous rock may form a large dome.

B. Now write sentences from the paragraph to label each photo. Then number the photos to make a sequence.

_____

_____

_____

_____

_____

_____

Unit 3: Lesson 2

More Review and Practice

VOCABULARY

Use the words in the box to identify each clue. Write the word on the line.

| erosion   glacier   earthquake   geologist   weathering |

1. I am a scientist who studies rocks.   _____

2. I am a big sheet of ice.   _____

3. I make the ground shake.   _____

4. I am the breaking of rock into pieces.   _____

5. I am the moving of soil and rocks.   _____

VOCABULARY IN CONTEXT

Complete the paragraph. Use words from the box. There is one extra word.

| weathering   earthquakes   geologist   glacier |

The earth's surface changes over time. **(1)** A _____ studies these

changes. He or she studies how wind, water, and animals break down rock. This is called

(2) _____. Geologists also study the movement of the earth's crust.

Strong movements are called **(3)** _____. They can cause a lot of damage.

CHECK YOUR UNDERSTANDING

Choose the best answer. Circle the letter.

1. An earthquake often happens along a _____.

    a. fault   **b.** road   **c.** volcano

2. A volcano erupts when _____.

    a. weathering occurs   **b.** a glacier melts   **c.** pressure builds

3. _____ can change the shape of the land.

    a. Erosion   **b.** Geologists   **c.** Animals

4. A tsunami can occur as a result of _____.

    a. a rock cycle   **b.** a glacier   **c.** an earthquake

Science Reading Strategy: Cause and Effect

Read the paragraph. Write the effects in the diagram.

   A mountaintop is a good place to see the effects of weathering.
Mountaintops are exposed to air, wind, and water. Over time, these forces
cause the rock surface to break up into pieces. Many mountains are covered by
plantlike things called lichens (LEYE-kuhnz). Lichens produce chemicals that
also cause rock to break apart.

Cause   **Effect**

| Mountaintops are exposed to air, wind, and water. | ➡ | |
| Many mountains are covered by lichens. | ➡ | |

Using Visuals: Photo Sequences

Look at the pictures below. Then answer the questions.

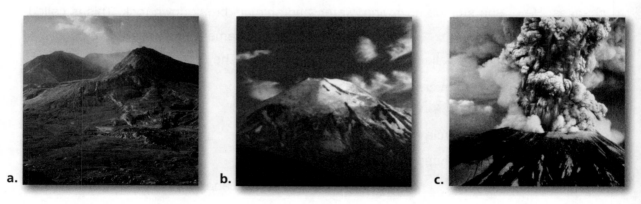

a.   b.   c.

1. These photos are not in the correct sequence. What is the correct sequence?

   _____

2. What does this photo sequence show?

   _____

Unit 3
Unit Review

VOCABULARY

Draw an arrow from each key word to words that tell about it. Write sentences.

1. weathering	rock formed when volcanoes erupt
2. igneous	solid substance that has crystals
3. mineral	big sheet of ice
4. erosion	rock that can have fossils in it
5. sedimentary	rock formed when rock changes
6. metamorphic	the moving of rocks and soil
7. properties	the breaking down of rock
8. glacier	traits

1. _____

2. _____

3. _____

4. _____

5. _____

6. _____

7. _____

8. _____

VOCABULARY IN CONTEXT

Complete each sentence. Use words from the box. There is one extra word.

metamorphic	glacier	weathering	properties	volcano	sedimentary

1. Each mineral has different _____.

2. A _____ carries rocks with it as it moves.

3. Birds and plants can cause _____.

4. An earthquake and a _____ are two strong forces of nature.

5. _____ rock is formed when heat and pressure cause rock to change.

Science Reading Strategy: Ask Questions

Read the paragraph below. Write questions using *What, Where, Why,* and *How.* Then write your answers.

Diamonds come from deep in the earth. They are carbon deposits that are exposed to heat and pressure over a very long time. That is why diamond crystals are so hard. Diamond crystals come closer to the surface through volcanic pipes. These are openings in old volcanoes. The hot liquid rock pushes the crystals up through the mantle toward the earth's crust.

Question Words	Questions and Answers
What	
Where	
Why	
How	

EXTENSION PROJECT

In this unit you learned about minerals and their properties. Choose one mineral to learn about its properties and how people use it. Write a paragraph about the mineral and its uses.

Unit 3: Unit Experiment

Experiment Log: How Do Rocks Change?

Follow the steps of the scientific method as you do your experiment. Write notes about each step as the experiment progresses.

Step 1: Ask questions.

Step 2: Make a hypothesis.

Step 3: Test your hypothesis.

Step 4: Observe.

Step 5: Draw conclusions.

Write About It

1. You learned about diamonds in this unit. What are some properties of diamonds? Why do you think people value them so highly?

2. Rocks are strong. But water can wear away rock over time. Write a story about a contest between two characters: Rock and Water. Which character is stronger?

Unit 4: Lesson 1

Before You Read

VOCABULARY

A. Draw an arrow from each key word to words that tell about it.

1. solar system	ball of ice and dust
2. atmosphere	a group of stars, planets, gases, and dust
3. galaxy	nine planets orbiting the sun
4. asteroids	move around the sun
5. comet	made of gases
6. orbit	pieces of rock and metal

B. Write four sentences below using a key word and the words that tell about it.

1. _____

2. _____

3. _____

4. _____

C. Circle the best word to complete each sentence.

1. The earth (orbits / gases) the sun.

2. A galaxy is a group of planets, (oxygen / stars), gases, and dust.

3. The atmosphere is made of (metals / gases).

4. A comet is a ball of dust and (stars / ice).

5. (Galaxies / Asteroids) are pieces of metal and rock.

D. Write T for *true* or F for *false*. Correct the sentences that are false.

_____ **1.** Galaxies orbit the sun.

_____ **2.** A comet is a ball of ice and dust.

_____ **3.** Gases make up a planet's atmosphere.

_____ **4.** Asteroids are groups of stars and planets.

_____ **5.** A solar system is a group of planets orbiting a sun.

Science Reading Strategy: Reread

A. Read the paragraph below. Then cover the paragraph. Answer question 1.

> The planet we live on is called Earth. Earth's atmosphere is made up of several gases. One of these gases is oxygen. People and other animals need oxygen to survive. Earth is just one of nine planets in our solar system. All the planets in our solar system orbit a bright star—the sun. Asteroids and comets are part of our solar system, too. They also orbit the sun.

1. What planet do we live on?

_____

B. Reread the paragraph. Answer the questions.

2. What important gas is part of Earth's atmosphere?

_____

3. What is Earth part of?

_____

4. How many planets are there in our solar system?

_____

5. Which objects orbit the sun?

_____

C. Reread the paragraph again. Write three sentences about Earth.

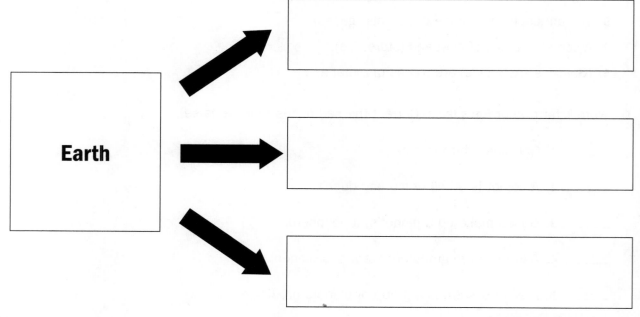

Unit 4: Lesson 1

Before You Read

SCIENCE SKILLS

Using Visuals: Illustrations

Look at the illustration of our solar system. Read the paragraph. Then answer the questions.

Illustrations are good tools for teaching about stars and planets. It isn't easy to take pictures of the planets in our solar system. Scientists have to use big telescopes with a special camera. The planets in our solar system are so far away from one another that even scientists cannot include them all in the same photo. But an artist can look at photos of each planet and use them as models. Then the artist draws or paints the nine planets together, as they appear in the solar system.

1. How do scientists take pictures of the planets in our solar system?

   _____

2. Why can't scientists include all nine planets in the same photo?

   _____

3. How can an artist use photos?

   _____

4. How many planets can you see in this picture?

   _____

5. Name the planets, moving from left to right.

   _____

Using Visuals: Illustrations

Look at the picture. Choose the best answer. Circle the letter.

1. This picture is _____.

   a. a photograph   **b.** a diagram   **c.** an illustration

2. This picture shows _____.

   a. a comet orbiting the sun   **b.** an asteroid hitting a planet   **c.** a volcano erupting on Mars

3. This event caused _____.

   a. fires   **b.** floods   **c.** ice storms

4. The planet in this picture is _____.

   a. Earth   **b.** Mars   **c.** Pluto

5. The event shown in this picture _____.

   a. never happened   **b.** happened recently   **c.** happened a long time ago

Unit 4: Lesson 1

More Review and Practice

VOCABULARY

Complete the puzzle. Use key words. Write the secret word.

1. The Milky Way is a _____.

2. _____ orbit the sun.

3. Earth has a(n) _____ around it.

4. A _____ is a ball of ice and dust.

5. Our _____ has nine planets.

Secret word: ___ ___ ___ ___ ___

VOCABULARY IN CONTEXT

Complete the paragraph. Use words from the box.

comets	galaxy	asteroids	solar system	atmosphere

Our **(1)** _____ is made up of nine planets with a sun in the center.

It belongs to a **(2)** _____ called the Milky Way. **(3)** _____

and **(4)** _____ are also part of our solar system. Earth is the only planet

whose **(5)** _____ contains oxygen.

CHECK YOUR UNDERSTANDING

Answer the questions.

1. In what galaxy do we live?

   _____

2. What do you call the path that each planet moves in?

   _____

3. What are the four planets closest to the sun?

   _____

4. What are the five planets farthest from the sun?

   _____

Science Reading Strategy: Reread

Answer the questions. If you can't answer them all, reread page 140 in your Student Book.

1. What are asteroids?

_____

2. Where do asteroids in our solar system orbit the sun?

_____

3. What are comets made of?

_____

4. What happens when the sun heats up a comet?

_____

5. Do comets reflect light from the sun or do they make their own light?

_____

Using Visuals: Illustrations

Look at the picture. Then answer the questions.

1. What does this illustration show? _____

2. What planets do you see? _____

3. To which solar system do these planets belong? _____

4. In what ways is this illustration not realistic? _____

_____

Unit 4: Lesson 2

Before You Read

VOCABULARY

A. Draw an arrow from each key word to words that tell about it.

1. constellation	everything in space
2. telescope	a star pattern
3. astronomers	a tool people use to see objects in space
4. universe	a very large number
5. trillion	scientists who study objects in space

B. Write five sentences using each key word and the words that tell about it.

1. _____

2. _____

3. _____

4. _____

5. _____

C. Write T for *true* or F for *false*. Correct the sentences that are false.

_____ **1.** Astronomers study rocks and minerals.

_____ **2.** Constellations are groups of stars that form patterns.

_____ **3.** The universe is everything in space.

_____ **4.** A telescope is a planet seen by astronomers.

_____ **5.** A trillion is a kind of asteroid.

D. Match the parts of the sentence. Write the letter.

_____ **1.** Leo the lion is a   **a.** number.

_____ **2.** Our solar system is part of the   **b.** scientists.

_____ **3.** Astronomers are   **c.** constellation.

_____ **4.** A telescope is used to observe   **d.** universe.

_____ **5.** A trillion is a very big   **e.** planets, stars, and galaxies.

Science Reading Strategy: Visualize

A. Read the paragraph below. As you read, make a picture in your mind of the universe.

The universe is everything in space. Space is a very dark place filled with stars, planets, comets, and galaxies. The stars can be different colors: red, orange, yellow, white, or blue. The Milky Way galaxy is the home of our solar system. It has a spiral shape. At the center is a ball. Coming out from the ball are long groups of stars called arms. The arms are curved because the whole galaxy is spinning.

B. Make an illustration showing how you visualized the universe.

Unit 4: Lesson 2

Before You Read

SCIENCE SKILLS

Science Reading Strategy: Visualize

Read the paragraph below. Visualize the stages in the life cycle of a star. Illustrate the stages in the boxes provided.

The stars in the universe do not live forever. Each star has a life cycle. It begins its life as a cloud of gases and dust. The gases and dust pull together. The cloud gets smaller, brighter, and hotter. Soon a new star is born. It is hot and bright, like our sun. In time, the star uses up most of its fuel. Then the star gets bigger, redder, and cooler. Finally the star gets so huge that it cannot hold onto its outer layers of gases. These gases form rings around the dying star. The star ends its life as a cloud of gases.

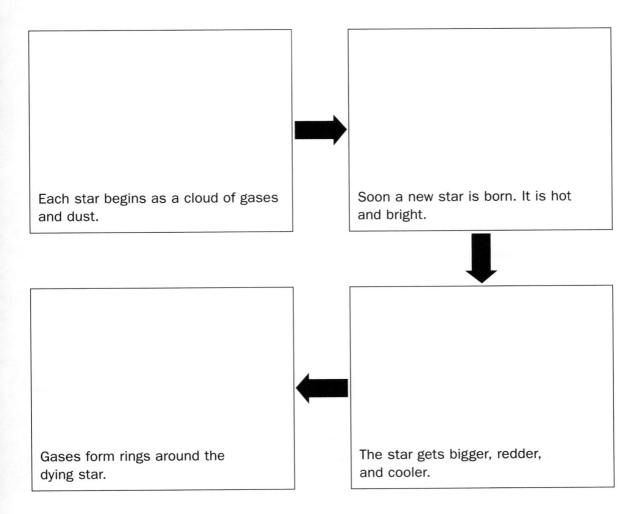

Each star begins as a cloud of gases and dust.

Soon a new star is born. It is hot and bright.

Gases form rings around the dying star.

The star gets bigger, redder, and cooler.

Using Visuals: Deep Space Photos

In the space below, draw a picture of the deep space photo on page 145 in your Student Book. Use the same colors as the photo. Then answer the questions.

1. What does the photo show?

   _____

2. Why are the objects in the photo so small?

   _____

3. What do the colors of the stars tell you?

   _____

4. Is your picture a photo, an illustration, or a diagram?

   _____

5. Is this a picture of the whole universe or just part of it? Explain.

   _____

Unit 4: Lesson 2

More Review and Practice

VOCABULARY

Use the words in the box to identify each clue. Write the word on the line.

constellation	trillion	astronomer	telescope	universe

1. I am a scientist who studies objects in space. _____

2. I have galaxies, stars, and planets in me. _____

3. I am a tool used to observe objects in space. _____

4. I am a very large number. _____

5. I am a group of stars that makes a pattern. _____

VOCABULARY IN CONTEXT

Write T for *true* or F for *false.* Correct the sentences that are false.

_____ **1.** An astronomer studies plants.

_____ **2.** The Hubble is a telescope in space.

_____ **3.** A constellation is a group of solar systems.

_____ **4.** There are many stars and planets in the universe.

CHECK YOUR UNDERSTANDING

Choose the best answer. Circle the letter.

1. A blue star is _____.

   a. very far away   **b.** very hot   **c.** very cool

2. There are two kinds of galaxies: spiral and _____.

   a. constellation   **b.** elliptical   **c.** Milky Way

3. Orion and Ursa Major are _____.

   a. cool stars   **b.** comets   **c.** constellations

4. _____ is everything in space, including galaxies and planets.

   a. The universe   **b.** A trillion   **c.** A comet

Science Reading Strategy: Visualize

Read the paragraph below. Visualize what the paragraph describes about Earth. Make an illustration below of the picture in your mind.

> The planet we live on is called Earth. Earth is an important part of our solar system. It is often called the blue planet because water covers more than 70 percent of Earth's surface. Our solar system is made up of eight more planets orbiting a bright star—our sun. Earth orbits the sun, too. It is the third planet from the sun.

Using Visuals: Deep Space Photos

Look at the deep space photo of the universe on page 149 in your Student Book. Then answer the questions below.

1. What do you see in the photo? _____

2. What different shapes of galaxies do you see? _____

3. What different colors do you see? _____

4. How can you tell that it is a deep space photo? _____

Unit 4
Unit Review

VOCABULARY

Draw an arrow from each key word to words that tell about it. Write sentences.

1. astronomer	patterns made by stars
2. universe	ball of ice and dust
3. comet	planets orbiting a sun
4. orbit	scientist who studies objects in space
5. solar system	everything in space
6. atmosphere	made up of gases
7. constellations	piece of rock and metal
8. asteroid	move around the sun

1. _____
2. _____
3. _____
4. _____
5. _____
6. _____
7. _____
8. _____

VOCABULARY IN CONTEXT

Complete the paragraph. Use words from the box. There is one extra word.

orbit	galaxy	astronomer	solar system	telescope	universe

    I learned many things in this unit. I learned that there are a large number of galaxies

in the (1) _____. I learned that an (2) _____ uses a

(3) _____ to observe objects in space. I also learned that our

(4) _____ is part of the Milky Way (5) _____.

Science Reading Strategy: Reread

A. Read the paragraph below. Then cover the paragraph. Answer the first question in a complete sentence.

The sun is at the center of our solar system. Every solar system has a star at its center. Our solar system is just a small part of the Milky Way galaxy. There are millions of solar systems in our galaxy. There are trillions of galaxies in the universe. The universe is a very, very, very large place.

1. What star is at the center of our solar system?

_____

B. Reread the paragraph. Answer the questions.

2. What does every solar system have at its center?

_____

3. What galaxy is our solar system part of?

_____

4. How many solar systems are in our galaxy?

_____

5. How many galaxies are in the universe?

_____

EXTENSION PROJECT

Sometimes an artist's illustration of an object is used instead of a photograph. Use a regular camera to take a picture of the moon. Compare your photo with the illustration of the moon on page 132 in your Student Book. Write a paragraph explaining which picture you prefer to use to study the moon. Why?

Unit 4: Unit Experiment

Experiment Log:
How Big Is the Solar System?

Follow the steps of the scientific method as you do your experiment. Write notes about each step as the experiment progresses.

Step 1: Ask questions.

Step 2: Make a hypothesis.

Step 3: Test your hypothesis.

Step 4: Observe.

Step 5: Draw conclusions.

Write About It

1. Think about these objects in space: comets, stars, planets, and asteroids. Which object is the most interesting to you? Write a paragraph about it.

2. Scientists have discovered ice on Mars. Some say, where there is water, there is life. Do you agree? Do you think there is or ever was life on Mars? Write a paragraph giving your opinion.

Unit 5: Lesson 1

Before You Read

VOCABULARY

A. Match each key word with words that tell about it. Write the letter.

_____ **1.** atoms   **a.** how much of something there is

_____ **2.** matter   **b.** the amount of mass in a given unit of volume

_____ **3.** mass   **c.** very tiny things that make up all matter

_____ **4.** density   **d.** anything that takes up space and has mass

_____ **5.** measure   **e.** the amount of space something takes up

_____ **6.** volume   **f.** find out how big or how heavy something is

B. Write four sentences using a key word and the words that tell about it.

1. _____

2. _____

3. _____

4. _____

C. Circle the best word to complete each sentence.

1. Anything that takes up space and has mass is (matter / density).

2. You need a powerful microscope to see (mass / atoms).

3. You use a balance to (matter / measure) the mass of an object.

4. The amount of space that an object takes up is its (mass / volume).

5. (Mass / Volume) is like weight.

D. Write T for *true* or F for *false.* Correct the sentences that are false.

_____ **1.** Atoms are very large things that make up matter.

_____ **2.** A cup of sand has more density than a cup of feathers.

_____ **3.** You can use a measuring cup to measure mass.

_____ **4.** You can use a balance to measure volume.

_____ **5.** Water takes up space and has mass.

Science Reading Strategy: Facts and Examples

Read the paragraph. Complete the diagram below with one more fact and an example for each.

All objects have mass, so all objects have density. But some objects are more dense than others. For example, suppose you throw a piece of wood in the water. It will float because wood has low density. Suppose you throw a piece of iron in the water. The iron will sink to the bottom because iron has high density.

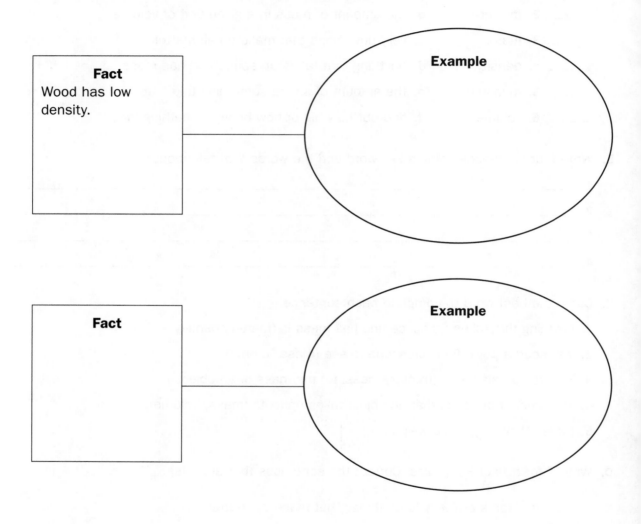

Fact
Wood has low density.

Example

Fact

Example

Unit 5: Lesson 1

Before You Read

Science Reading Strategy: Facts and Examples

Read the paragraph. Complete the diagram below.

Everything around you is matter. Your desk, your classmates, and the air you breathe are all examples of matter. There are many different kinds of matter, but all matter is made up of atoms. Atoms are very tiny. Suppose you made a tiny dot with your pencil, no bigger than the period at the end of this sentence. Millions of atoms could fit on such a tiny dot. Each kind of matter has its own properties. For example, water is clear and has no color. It is a liquid. It freezes at 0° Celsius and boils at 100° Celsius.

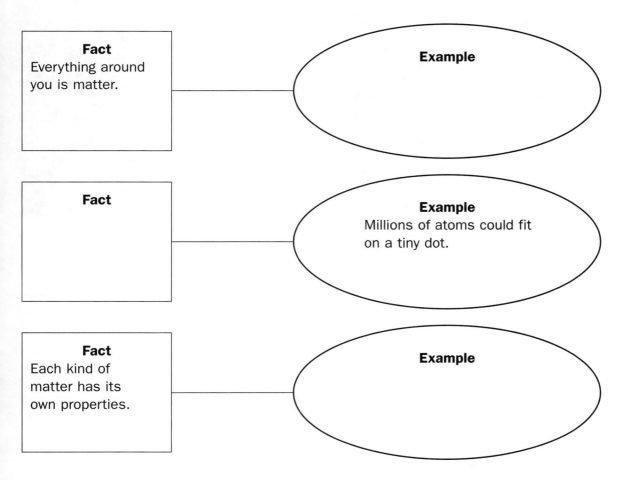

Fact
Everything around you is matter.

Example

Fact

Example
Millions of atoms could fit on a tiny dot.

Fact
Each kind of matter has its own properties.

Example

Using Visuals: Micrographs

Look at the micrographs of sugar, a snowflake, salt, and sand. Then answer the questions.

▲ Sugar

▲ Snowflake

▲ Salt

▲ Sand

1. Which substance is made of tiny rocks?

_____

2. Which substances can you eat?

_____

3. Which substance is a crystal with six branches?

_____

4. Which micrograph was easiest to recognize?

_____

5. Which is your favorite micrograph? Why?

_____

Unit 5: Lesson 1

More Review and Practice

VOCABULARY

Complete the puzzle. Use key words. Write the secret word.

1. _____ is like weight.

2. Everything around you is _____.

3. A cup of pennies has more _____ than a cup of popcorn.

4. _____ are tiny things.

5. _____ can be measured in liters.

6. We use a balance to _____ mass.

Secret word: ___ ___ ___ ___ ___ ___

VOCABULARY IN CONTEXT

Complete the paragraph. Use words from the box. There is one extra word.

matter	volume	measure	density	atoms	mass

All **(1)** _____ is made of tiny things called **(2)** _____.

We can **(3)** _____ the mass, **(4)** _____,

and **(5)** _____ of different kinds of matter.

CHECK YOUR UNDERSTANDING

Choose the best answer. Circle the letter.

1. Matter can be living or _____.

   a. hard   **b.** nonliving   **c.** space

2. Color, shape, and size are _____ you can see.

   a. balloons   **b.** containers   **c.** properties

3. A salad is a _____ of different kinds of matter.

   a. mixture   **b.** mass   **c.** volume

4. _____ is an example of a pure substance.

   a. Sand   **b.** Salt   **c.** Chocolate milk

Science Reading Strategy: Facts and Examples

Use the information in the paragraph to complete the diagram.

Each type of matter has its own properties. For example, honey is sweet and it is a liquid. Because honey is a liquid, it shares properties with other liquids. You can pour honey, and it takes the shape of its container.

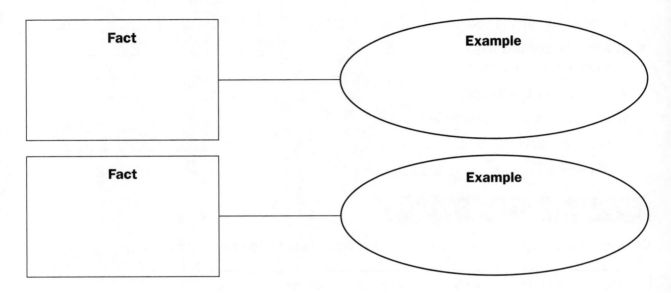

Using Visuals: Micrographs

Look at the micrographs of atoms on pages 165, 175, and 177 in your Student Book. Then answer the questions.

1. Look at the micrograph on page 165. What substance do those atoms make?

   _____

2. Look at the micrograph on page 175. What substance do those atoms make?

   _____

3. Look at the micrograph on page 177. What substance do those atoms make?

   _____

4. Draw and label the shapes of the atoms in each micrograph.

Unit 5: Lesson 2

Before You Read

VOCABULARY

A. Match each key word to words that tell about it. Write the letter.

_____ **1.** physical change   **a.** forms of matter: solid, liquid, and gas

_____ **2.** chemical change   **b.** the temperature at which a solid melts

_____ **3.** boiling point   **c.** the groups of atoms in the matter do not change

_____ **4.** states   **d.** the groups of atoms in the matter change

_____ **5.** melting point   **e.** the temperature at which a liquid changes to a gas

B. Write five sentences using each key word and the words that tell about it.

1. _____

2. _____

3. _____

4. _____

5. _____

C. Circle the best word to complete each sentence.

1. The three (states / points) of matter are solid, liquid, and gas.

2. A solid changes to a liquid at its (boiling / melting) point.

3. A liquid changes to a gas at its (boiling / melting) point.

4. Mashing corn is an example of a (physical / chemical) change.

5. Rusting metal is an example of a (physical / chemical) change.

D. Write T for *true* or F for *false*. Correct the sentences that are false.

_____ **1.** There are three states of matter: solid, liquid, and space.

_____ **2.** Water vapor is a gas.

_____ **3.** The boiling point of water is 0° Celsius.

_____ **4.** When ice melts, water changes from a solid to a liquid.

_____ **5.** Water changing states is a chemical change.

Science Reading Strategy: Idea Maps

Complete the idea map below with ideas you learned in Lesson 1.

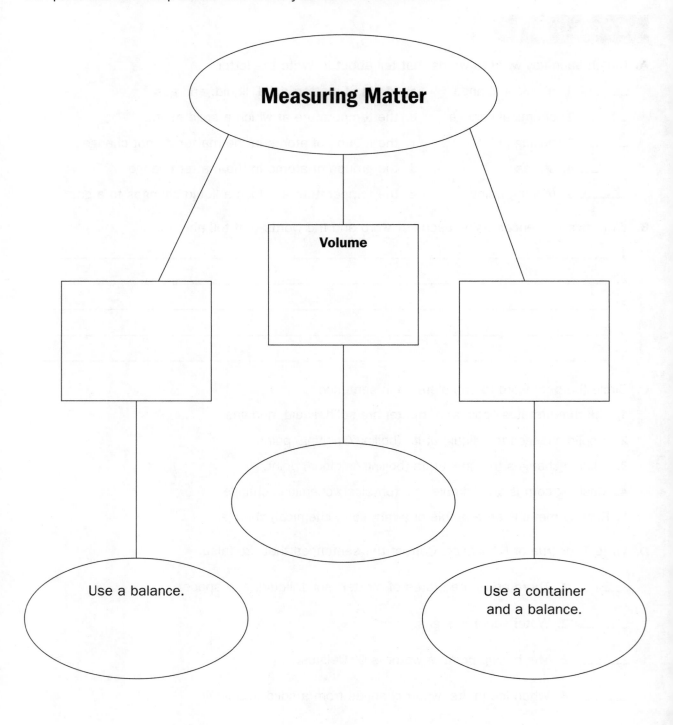

Measuring Matter

Volume

Use a balance.

Use a container
and a balance.

Unit 5: Lesson 2

Before You Read

SCIENCE SKILLS

Science Reading Strategy: Idea Maps

Complete the idea map below with two kinds of matter for each of the three states.

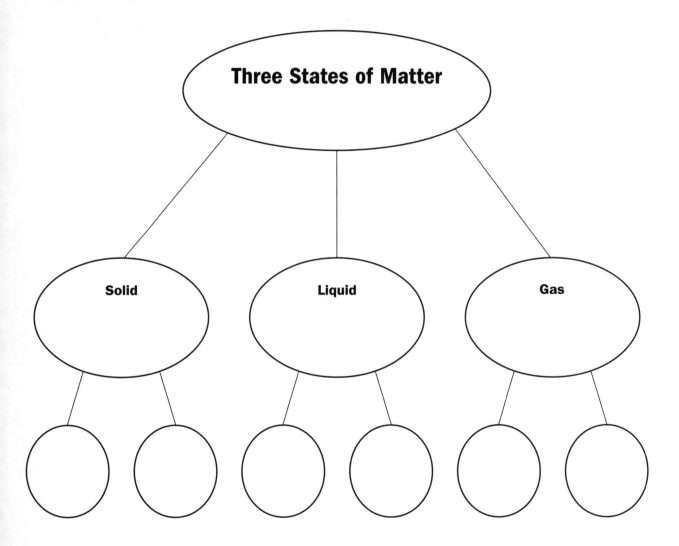

Using Visuals: States of Matter Illustrations

Look at the illustrations below. Then answer the questions.

_____ _____ _____

1. Which state of matter does each illustration show? Label the illustrations.

   _____

2. What does each round shape represent?

   _____

3. In which state of matter is there the most space between atoms?

   _____

4. In which state is there the least space between atoms?

   _____

5. How would you change a liquid into a gas?

   _____

Unit 5: Lesson 2

More Review and Practice

VOCABULARY

Use words from the box to identify each clue. Write the word or phrase on the line.

| chemical change | melting point | physical change | states | boiling point |

1. I am the temperature at which a liquid changes to a gas. _____

2. I change groups of atoms to make a new type of matter. _____

3. I am the temperature at which a solid changes to a liquid. _____

4. I change only the way matter looks. _____

5. I am also called forms of matter. _____

VOCABULARY IN CONTEXT

Complete the paragraph. Use words from the box.

| boiling point | chemical change | states | melting point | physical change |

There are three **(1)** _____ of matter: solid, liquid, and gas. These
three forms of matter can change. For example, at the **(2)** _____,
ice changes to liquid. At the **(3)** _____, water changes to vapor,
or steam. Matter can change in two main ways. Corn can be mashed. That is a
(4) _____. A metal chain can rust. That is a **(5)** _____.

CHECK YOUR UNDERSTANDING

Choose the best answer. Circle the letter.

1. The atoms in a _____ move around freely.

    a. solid   **b.** liquid   **c.** chemical

2. A rise in _____ causes atoms to move faster.

    a. temperature   **b.** density   **c.** mass

3. The digestion of food is an example of a _____.

    a. physical change   **b.** boiling point   **c.** chemical change

Science Reading Strategy: Idea Maps

Complete the idea map with ideas from this lesson.

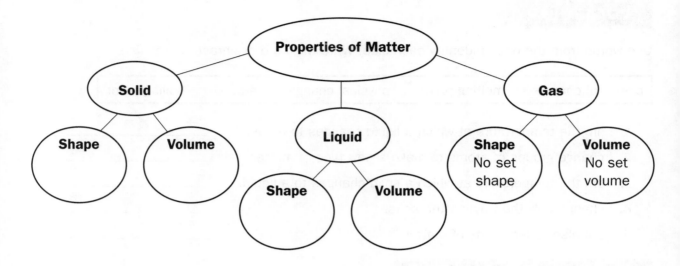

Using Visuals: States of Matter Illustrations

Look at the illustrations below. Then answer the questions.

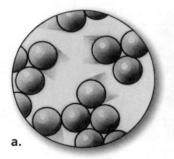

a.

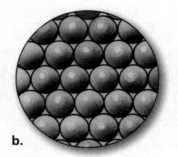

b.

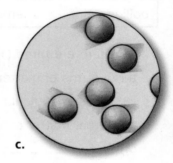

c.

1. What is illustration a. an example of?

   _____

2. What is illustration b. an example of?

   _____

3. What is illustration c. an example of?

   _____

4. In which state do the atoms move the fastest?

   _____

5. In which state do the atoms move the slowest?

   _____

Unit 5
Unit Review

VOCABULARY

Draw an arrow from each key word to words that tell about it. Write sentences.

1. chemical change		very tiny things that make up matter
2. physical change		temperature at which a solid melts
3. density		the space matter takes up
4. melting point		temperature at which a liquid boils
5. volume		mass per unit of volume
6. atoms		a different kind of matter is formed
7. boiling point		matter changes shape or state
8. mass		how much of something there is

1. _____

2. _____

3. _____

4. _____

5. _____

6. _____

7. _____

8. _____

VOCABULARY IN CONTEXT

Complete the paragraph. Use words from the box.

volume	atoms	mass	matter	measure

    (1) _____ are tiny things that make up **(2)** _____.

You can **(3)** _____ the properties of matter, including

(4) _____ and **(5)** _____.

Science Reading Strategy: Facts and Examples

Read the paragraph. Complete the diagram.

Most things in nature are mixtures. Examples include sand, ocean water, and soil. Anything you can combine is a mixture. Suppose you mix chocolate powder and milk. It forms a mixture.

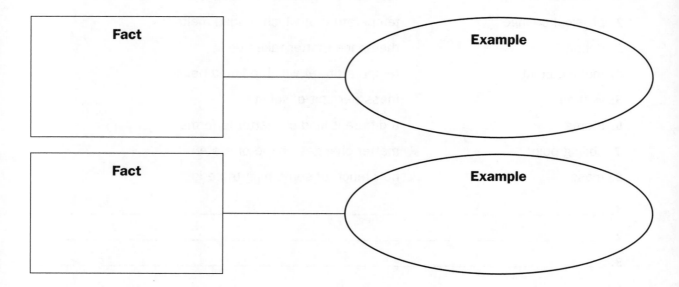

EXTENSION PROJECT

We know that ice melts, or changes from a solid to a liquid, at 0° Celsius. We also know that water boils, or changes from a liquid to a gas, at 100° Celsius. Research the melting and boiling points of five other substances. How do these melting and boiling points compare to those of water?

Unit 5: Unit Experiment

Experiment Log:
Can You Observe Density?

Follow the steps of the scientific method as you do your experiment. Write notes about each step as the experiment progresses.

Step 1: Ask questions.

Step 2: Make a hypothesis.

Step 3: Test your hypothesis.

Step 4: Observe.

Step 5: Draw conclusions.

Write About It

1. Physical and chemical changes are happening around you all the time. Write about physical and chemical changes you have personally observed. What happened in each change?

2. Write about the foods you eat. Which foods are mixtures? Which foods can change from one state to another? Give examples.

Unit 6: Lesson 1

Before You Read

VOCABULARY

A. Match each key word with words that tell about it. Write the letter.

_____ 1. echo	**a.** how fast or slow the air vibrates
_____ 2. pitch	**b.** sound heard again
_____ 3. sound waves	**c.** how soft or loud a sound is
_____ 4. frequency	**d.** movements up and down
_____ 5. volume	**e.** vibrations that move through the air
_____ 6. vibrations	**f.** how high or low a sound is

B. Write six sentences using each key word and the words that tell about it.

1. _____
2. _____
3. _____
4. _____
5. _____
6. _____

C. Read the clues. Write key words.

1. I am vibrations that travel through the air. What am I?

   _____

2. I am the loudness or softness of sound. What am I?

   _____

3. I am a sound that you hear again and again. What am I?

   _____

4. I am how low or high a sound is. What am I?

   _____

5. I am how fast or slow the air vibrates. What am I?

   _____

Science Reading Strategy: Act It Out

You learned that sound travels in waves. Read the paragraph. Act it out with several classmates.

   If you throw a rock into the water, you will see waves moving away from the center. The waves near the center are closer together. As they move away from the center, the waves get farther apart. The same thing happens with sound. The closer you are to the source of a sound, the louder the sound will be. The farther away you are from the source, the softer the sound will be. Stand outside with your classmates. Have your classmates placed around you at different distances and shout loudly. Who can hear you the best? Who can't hear you as well?

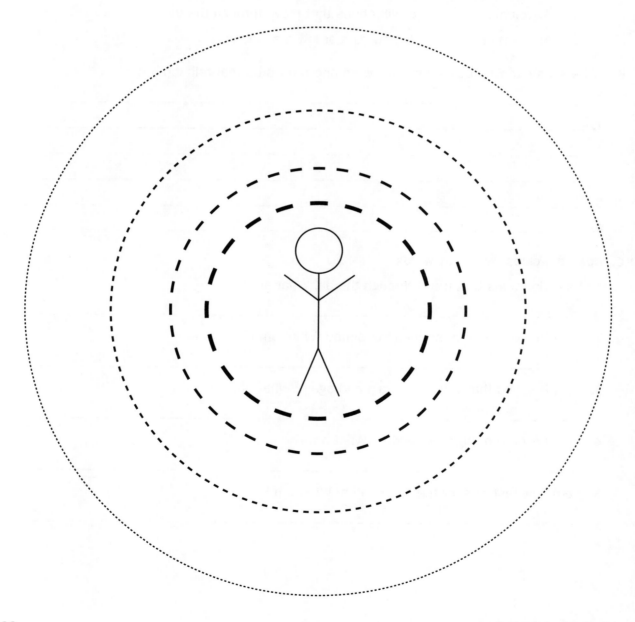

Unit 6: Lesson 1

Before You Read

SCIENCE SKILLS

Using Visuals: Charts

Look at the charts. Compare and contrast the volume of various sounds. Then answer the questions.

Sound	Volume in Decibels
Plane taking off	150
Motorcycle	100
TV	70
Rain	50
Mosquito	20
Breathing	10

Sound	Volume in Decibels
Shuttle taking off	190
Rock concert	115
Busy street	70
Classroom or office	45
Falling leaves	10

1. Which sounds have the same volume in decibels?

   _____

2. Which sound has the highest volume?

   _____

3. Which sound is louder, falling leaves or rain?

   _____

4. How many decibels louder is a rock concert than a TV?

   _____

5. What decibel levels do you think are dangerous to your hearing?

   _____

Using Visuals: Charts

Look at the chart. Compare and contrast the hearing ranges of humans and other animals. Then answer the questions.

Species	Approximate Frequency Range of Hearing
Human	20–23,000 Hz
Bat	2,000–110,000 Hz
Beluga whale	1,000–123,000 Hz
Chicken	125–2,000 Hz
Dog	67–45,000 Hz
Dolphin	75–150,000 Hz

Hz=hertz (a unit of frequency)

1. Which animal's range of hearing is closest to a human's?

   _____

2. Which animal can hear sounds of the lowest frequency?

   _____

3. Which animal has the widest range of hearing?

   _____

4. Of the bat and the beluga whale, which animal has a wider range of hearing?

   _____

5. How does the chicken's hearing range compare to that of the other animals on the chart?

   _____

Unit 6: Lesson 1

More Review and Practice

VOCABULARY

Complete the puzzle. Use key words. Write the secret word.

1. _____ is measured in decibels.

2. A whistle makes a high _____ wave.

3. _____ move out in all directions.

4. _____ make sounds.

5. An _____ is a repeated sound.

Secret word: ___ ___ ___ ___ ___

VOCABULARY IN CONTEXT

Complete the paragraph. Use words from the box. There is one extra word.

pitch	echo	volume	vibrations	frequency

(1) _____ is how high or low a sound is. It is caused by the

(2) _____ of the sound waves. A tuba makes low-frequency

(3) _____, so the sound it creates has a low pitch. Low sounds

can be loud or soft. When a tuba player blows a lot of air into the horn, he or she

makes a sound with a loud (4) _____.

CHECK YOUR UNDERSTANDING

Choose the best answer. Circle the letter.

1. Pitch is caused by the _____ of the sound waves.

   a. frequency   **b.** volume   **c.** echo

2. Sound waves _____ out in all directions.

   a. throw   **b.** dance   **c.** move

3. Soft objects like carpets _____ sound waves.

   a. echo   **b.** repeat   **c.** absorb

4. Sound waves that are close together make a _____ sound.

   a. low-pitch   **b.** high-pitch   **c.** low-volume

Science Reading Strategy: Act It Out

Read the paragraph. Act it out. Then answer the questions.

An echo occurs when a sound hits a hard surface and the waves bounce back. Use a small ball to act out this statement. Try throwing the ball against different types of hard surfaces.

1. Is there always an echo against any hard surface?

_____

2. What would happen if the ball hit a pillow? Would there be an echo?

_____

Using Visuals: Charts

Read the chart. Then answer the questions.

Matter	Speed of Sound	
	Meters per second	**Feet per second**
Dry, cold air	343	1,125
Water	1,550	5,085
Hard wood	3,960	12,992
Glass	4,540	14,895
Steel	5,050	16,568

1. In which kind of matter does sound travel the fastest?

_____

2. In which kind of matter does sound travel the slowest?

_____

3. Which kinds of matter are solids?

_____

4. Does sound travel faster in water or in glass? Why?

_____

5. Why does sound travel faster in steel than in dry, cold air?

_____

Unit 6: Lesson 2

Before You Read

VOCABULARY

A. Match each key word with words that tell about it. Write the letter.

_____ **1.** reflection   **a.** the bending of light

_____ **2.** refraction   **b.** the bouncing of light waves off a surface

_____ **3.** transparent   **c.** light is one type

_____ **4.** translucent   **d.** you can see through it

_____ **5.** opaque   **e.** you cannot see through it clearly

_____ **6.** electromagnetic wave **f.** light cannot pass through it

B. Write six sentences using each key word and the words that tell about it.

1. _____

2. _____

3. _____

4. _____

5. _____

6. _____

C. Write T for *true* or F for *false*. Correct the sentences that are false.

_____ **1.** Transparent objects reflect light.

_____ **2.** Translucent objects allow some light to pass through them.

_____ **3.** Electromagnetic waves have their own energy.

_____ **4.** The moon is a translucent object.

_____ **5.** When light waves bounce off a surface, we call it refraction.

_____ **6.** We can see through transparent objects.

_____ **7.** Opaque means that light cannot pass through it.

_____ **8.** Light is a type of sound wave.

SCIENCE SKILLS

Science Reading Strategy: Draw a Picture

A. Read the definition of reflection. Draw a picture below to represent it.

Light waves bounce off the surface of opaque objects like the moon. We can see the moon because it reflects the sun's light. This is called reflection.

B. Show your picture to a partner. Talk about your picture.

Unit 6: Lesson 2

Before You Read

SCIENCE SKILLS

Science Reading Strategy: Draw a Picture

A. Read the paragraph. Draw a picture below of the underlined sentences.

Electromagnetic waves are all around you. Light is a kind of electromagnetic wave. When you go to the beach, the sun's ultraviolet (UV) rays can burn your skin. <u>UV rays come to you in waves and hit your skin repeatedly. You cannot see these waves, but you can feel the heat. If you stay too long under the sun, these light waves will "cook" you.</u>

B. Show your picture to a partner. Talk about your picture.

Using Visuals: Wave Diagrams

Look at the wave diagram of the electromagnetic spectrum. Then answer the questions.

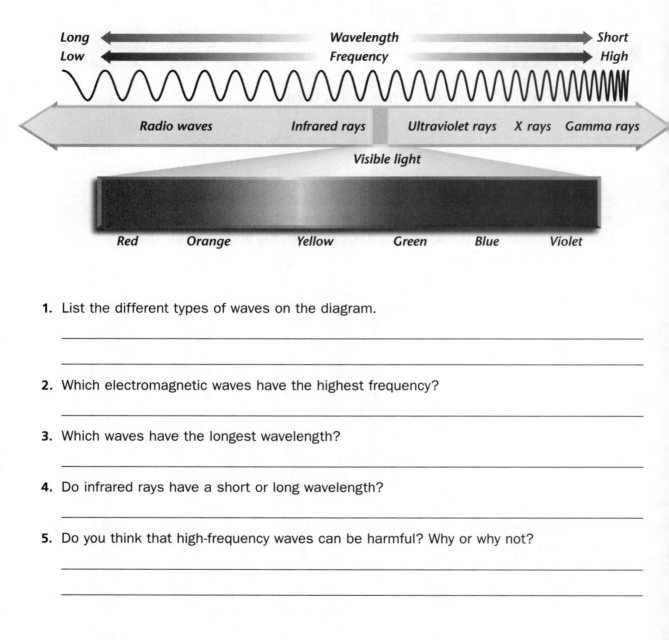

1. List the different types of waves on the diagram.

   _____

   _____

2. Which electromagnetic waves have the highest frequency?

   _____

3. Which waves have the longest wavelength?

   _____

4. Do infrared rays have a short or long wavelength?

   _____

5. Do you think that high-frequency waves can be harmful? Why or why not?

   _____

   _____

Unit 6: Lesson 2
More Review and Practice

VOCABULARY

Use words from the box to identify each clue. Write the word on the line.

| reflection | refraction | opaque | electromagnetic waves | transparent |

1. I am the bending of light.   _____

2. I don't let light go through me.   _____

3. I am visible light, X rays, and radio waves.   _____

4. You can see through me.   _____

5. I am light waves bouncing off surfaces.   _____

VOCABULARY IN CONTEXT

Circle the best answer to complete each sentence.

Light is (**1.** a sound / an electromagnetic) wave. Water drops can make a rainbow by (**2.** reflecting / refracting) light. The drops of water separate the sunlight into different wavelengths. But water can also cause a (**3.** reflection / refraction). Think of looking into smooth water on a lake. You can see yourself. Some water is (**4.** opaque / transparent), and you can see to the bottom. Other water might have mud in it. You cannot see through it clearly. It is (**5.** transparent / translucent).

CHECK YOUR UNDERSTANDING

Choose the best answer. Circle the letter.

1. Toasters use _____ rays to toast waffles.

   a. opaque   **b.** ultraviolet   **c.** infrared

2. Electromagnetic waves have their own _____ and magnetic energy.

   a. transparent   **b.** electrical   **c.** wavy

3. The color of light depends on its _____ and frequency.

   a. refraction   **b.** wavelength   **c.** reflection

4. You can't see a reflection of yourself on _____ surface.

   a. an uneven   **b.** an even   **c.** a hard

Science Reading Strategy: Draw a Picture

Find an object that is mostly one color. Draw a picture of this object absorbing and reflecting the different wavelengths of light.

Using Visuals: Wave Diagrams

Look at the wave diagrams on page 225 in your Student Book. Then answer the questions.

1. What happens when light waves hit a smooth surface?

_____

2. Which wave diagram shows what happens when light waves hit a mirror's surface?

_____

3. Which wave diagram shows what happens when light hits the surface of your clothing?

_____

Unit 6

Unit Review

VOCABULARY

Draw an arrow from each key word to words that tell about it. Write sentences.

1. electromagnetic waves	how soft or loud a sound is
2. pitch	light waves cannot travel through
3. frequency	light waves bouncing off a surface
4. reflection	how close together or far apart sound waves are
5. refraction	how low or high a sound is
6. vibrations	have their own energy
7. volume	the bending of light
8. opaque	movements up and down

1. _____

2. _____

3. _____

4. _____

5. _____

6. _____

7. _____

8. _____

VOCABULARY IN CONTEXT

Complete the paragraph. Use words from the box. There is one extra word.

reflection	volume	refraction	transparent	opaque	pitch

    Nature offers much to see and hear. A cricket's sound has a high

(1) _____. Many crickets together make the **(2)** _____

of the sound loud. Look at a rainbow, and you see **(3)** _____ at work.

The water droplets bend the light. Sometimes you see your **(4)** _____

in a pool of water. Its smooth surface is like a mirror. Have you ever seen a dragonfly's

wings? They are as **(5)** _____ as glass.

Science Reading Strategies: Act It Out and Draw a Picture

In this unit you learned that light can be separated by water drops. Fill a spray bottle with water. As you spray the water, shine a flashlight through the drops. Write what you see.

_____

_____

_____

_____

_____

Now draw a picture of what you saw.

EXTENSION PROJECT

Write a poem about interesting sounds and sights. Include ideas that you learned in this unit.

Unit 6: Unit Experiment

Experiment Log: How Does Light Reflect and Refract?

Follow the steps of the scientific method as you do your experiment. Write notes about each step as the experiment progresses.

Step 1: Ask questions.

Step 2: Make a hypothesis.

Step 3: Test your hypothesis.

Step 4: Observe.

Data Table	
Step	**Observation**
1.	
2.	
3.	
4.	

Step 5: Draw conclusions.

Write About It

1. Write a hypothesis about the relationship between the different light colors and the colors of the coolest and hottest stars. Look at the electromagnetic spectrum diagram on page 216 or 220 in your Student Book to help you write your hypothesis.

2. In your opinion, which is more important—to be able to see objects or to hear sounds? Write a paragraph giving your opinion.

Credits

GETTING STARTED 1 left, L. Clarke/Bettmann/CORBIS; 1 middle, Prentice Hall School Division; 1 right, Christine M. Douglas/Dorling Kindersley; 3 top left, Gail Shumway/Taxi/Getty Images; 3 top middle, Photri/Stock Market/CORBIS; 3 top right, Monique le Luhandre/Dorling Kindersley; 3 bottom left, Peter Ardito/Index Stock Imagery; 3 bottom middle, NASA; 3 bottom right, Mark Green/Taxi/Getty Images; 7 top left, Photodisc/Getty Images; 7 top middle, Mike Dunning/Dorling Kindersley; 7 top right, © 1991 Paul Silverman/Fundamental Photographs, NYC; 7 middle left, Steve Cole/Photodisc/Getty Images; 7 middle middle, Ryan McVay/Photodisc/Getty Images; 7 middle right, Andy Crawford/Dorling Kindersley; 7 bottom left, Steve Cole/Photodisc/Getty Images; 7 bottom right, Pearson Learning Photo Studio; 11 top left, Jacob Halaska/Index Stock Imagery; 11 top middle, Peter Gardner/Dorling Kindersley; 11 top right, W. Geiersperger/Bettmann/CORBIS; 11 bottom left, Courtesy of Ohaus Corporation; 11 bottom middle, Ryan McVay/Photodisc/Getty Images; 11 bottom right, Peter Ardito/Index Stock Imagery; 13 top left, Walter Stuart; 13 top right, Marli Miller; 13 bottom, Jon Weiman/Spots on the Spot; 14 top left, Network Graphics/Pearson Education/Prentice Hall College Division; 14 top right, Dorling Kindersley; 14 bottom right, Tom Leonard.

Unit 1 19, © Nigel Cattlin/H.S.I./Photo Researchers, Inc.; 20 left, Laurie O'Keefe/Pearson Education/ Prentice Hall College Division; 20 right, Walter Stuart; 22, Tom Leonard; 25 left, James Stevenson/Dorling Kindersley; 25 right, Neil Fletcher and Matthew Ward/Dorling Kindersley; 26, Simone End/Dorling Kindersley; 30 left, Laurie O'Keefe/Pearson Education/Prentice Hall College Division; 30 right, © Nigel Cattlin/H.S.I./Photo Researchers, Inc..

Unit 2 35 left, Martin Harvey/Peter Arnold, Inc.; 35 right, Jacques Jangoux/Peter Arnold, Inc.; 36, Bob Daemmrich/Bob Daemmrich Photography, Inc.; 38, Nancy Wolff/Omni-Photo Communications, Inc.; 40, Martin Harvey/Peter Arnold, Inc.; 46, Jeff Hunter/Image Bank/Getty Images.

Unit 3 52, Dorling Kindersley; 58 top left, © Doug Perrine/DRK Photo; 58 top right, Joanna McCarthy/ Image Bank/Getty Images; 58 bottom, Glen Allison/Photodisc/Getty Images; 60 left, Harry Glicken/David A. Johnston Cascades Volcano Observatory, Vancouver, WA/US Geological Survey/United States Department of the Interior; 60 middle, Washington State Tourism Development Division; 60 right, InterNetwork Media/ Photodisc/Getty Images.

Unit 4 67, John Hovell; 68, David A. Hardy/Photo Researchers, Inc.; 70, Chris Bjornberg/Photo Researchers, Inc.

Unit 5 84 top left, Andrew Syred/Allstock/Getty Images; 84 top right, Richard Walters/Visuals Unlimited; 84 bottom left, © 1993 Paul Silverman/Fundamental Photographs, NYC; 84 bottom right, Marli Miller; 90, Morgan Cain & Associates; 92, Ricky Blakeley/Dorling Kindersley.

Unit 6 106, Martucci Design.